F-000

85

MW00559727

# Lifelines

**Meditations for Everyday Life**

**Jake Kincaid**

Pages designed by Rebecca Jones.

Published by

Library Partners Press

ZSR Library

Wake Forest University

Winston-Salem, North Carolina 27106

www.librarypartnerspress.org

a digital publishing imprint

© 2014 by Jake Kincaid

All Rights Reserved.

# Lifelines

# Contents

# Preface

*Lifelines* was originally a series of meditations broadcast on local radio stations over a thirteen-year period in my thirty-year career as a parish minister. My hope was that the series would speak to human experience generally and appeal to people broadly on a wide range of topics, using diverse sources of inspiration. My aim was to prompt reflection and to encourage the human effort to find meaning and live well.

I selected the title of the series with two meanings in mind. The first meaning is expressed by Webster's definition of the word *lifeline.* A lifeline is "a line or rope for saving life." It is "something to grasp when there is danger of falling or being washed away." I hope in some meaningful way *Lifelines* has this life-saving benefit.

But I chose the title *Lifelines* with a second meaning of the word lifeline in mind. What aid and assistance *Lifelines* may convey is necessarily through the lines we humans are given in the drama of life itself. Help and hope are translated in the very words spoken to us across the ages and repeated in our present conversations with one another. For this reason, the meditations that follow are almost always based upon lines from poets and playwrights, songsters and comic strip characters, famous and ordinary people spoken to us in their own voices.

These lifelines are, not only lines for saving life, but also lines of daily dialogue.

Edward Smith Ufford, who lived from 1851 until 1929 through some of the most perilous times in history, wrote in 1884:

Throw out the lifeline, throw out the lifeline,
Someone is sinking today.

This printed version of *Lifelines,* like the original series, is meant for all who know from time to time the struggle to keep afloat and for all who wish to find aid for themselves and their companions.

# Reader's Guide

The meditations that follow are not organized according to any schedule of readings—daily, weekly, or monthly. Although the meditations on seasonal themes generally follow the calendar year, *Lifelines* is intended to be read leisurely—without haste, deliberately, with continued and extended thought. An alphabetical list of titles is provided at the end of the manuscript.

# Lifelines

# Gloom Bloomers

In an old garden book, there is a chapter entitled "Flowers that Grow in the Gloom." The chapter lists and describes plants that require little sunlight to grow and prosper better in the shade.

Likewise, in life there are qualities of character that emerge only as a result of adversity. Under favorable conditions, they fail to appear. Like the flowers and foliage of plants that grow in the gloom, these strengths and abilities of the soul abound only under the stress of inhospitable circumstances.

If flowers can grow in the gloom, we, too, can blossom in life's desert places. And if we can, then what for us was gloom can become what for us is glory.

# Two-Faced

January takes its name from the Roman god Janus. The Romans pictured Janus as a figure with two faces, one looking backward and the other looking forward.

The New Year is a time to look in two directions. It is a valuable time to look back, to review the past, to examine the path life has taken.

And it is an appropriate time to look ahead, to dream and to hope and to make plans. Perhaps, a time to change course.

With the approach of the New Year, take time to look both directions, backward and forward.

# Happy to Fail

Thomas Edison was one of the greatest inventors of all times. He is credited with 1,093 inventions, including the motion picture camera, the phonograph, and the electric light.

His secret? Perseverance. It is reported that he never let failure discourage him. When some 10,000 experiments with a storage battery failed, a friend tried to console him. "Why, I have not failed," Edison replied. "I've just found 10,000 ways that won't work."

Edison was happy to fail, for with every failure, he knew he was closer than before to a solution. Never fear failure.

# Commitments

The New Year is a time for examining our lives and commitments. What now are our priorities?

It's quite easy, really, in the course of living to get off track. Our priorities quickly become distorted. To borrow a line from the poet Alfred, Lord Tennyson, the New Year is a time to:

Ring out the false, ring in the true.

Indeed, what better time of year is there than the beginning of the New Year to evaluate our commitments and get them once again in the right order.

4

# Death Sentence

It is a phrase we associate with punishment of the worst forms of criminality, with the fates of traitors and terrorists, serial killers and calculating murderers. But the truth is that every person, the good and evil alike, lives under a death sentence. The biblical author, however much we wish he weren't, is simply right when in stark realism he writes, ". . . it is appointed for mortals to die once, . . ."

Much in life, if not most of life, is uncertain, but this one reality is sure: death. Little if anything is gained in denial of death's reality, although much of modern life is a reflection of the human inclination to avoid this unpleasant thought. But avoidance is short-sighted and, perhaps, even costly.

Some ancient Greek philosophers believed, on the contrary, that much is gained in acceptance of the fact of death. It is death, actually, which teaches us how best to live. Death provides viewpoint and teaches value as no other reality of life can or does.

The death sentence, under which every person lives, then, may well be the inspiration of every person's life strategy and the inspiration of a life well-lived.

# Sound Advice

A firm in Cincinnati that helps businesses become more productive suggests this philosophy for dealing with employee mistakes:

The firm says that it's good mental health to believe:

1. All people make mistakes. So expect mistakes.
2. People don't intend to make mistakes.
3. People don't like to make mistakes.
4. People want to "make up" for mistakes made.
5. People want to learn from their mistakes.

Sounds like good mental health, not just for businesses, but for everyone. Mistakes are a part of life. Here is sound advice for us all.

# At the Start of a New Year

Each New Year brings both promise and uncertainty. What lies ahead is never clear.

But the source of our strength for meeting any challenge is always sure. Our hope for the coming year is the same as every year before, indeed, none other than our help in past ages. God's outstretched arms extend across the days and weeks and months to support and sustain all who welcome their embrace.

There's nothing ahead we need fear.

# Inventory

The New Year is a time for taking stock—a time for examining the patterns our lives have been weaving. Where are we going in life? Do we have our priorities in their proper order? What kind of people are we becoming?

This kind of periodic self-examination is not a luxury but a necessity. Life has a tendency to get out of hand. Occasional adjustment is required to stay on course. A rearrangement of our loves and loyalties into their right order is necessary if we are to continue in the right direction.

Businesses periodically take inventory, listing what stock remains on hand and calculating the value of goods. What better time than the New Year to examine the array of our commitments with a serious intention of eliminating whatever among them is counterfeit or improper and to replace them with those that are truly important and worthwhile.

# What's a Lifetime?

The children of the comic strip *The Family Circus* from time to time wrestle with the most profound subjects. In an installment, the following conversation occurs.

"What does a lifetime consist of Billy?"

"It's usually a lot of 'yesterdays,' no 'tomorrows' and part of a 'today.'"

How quickly a lifetime passes. The only portion in our grasp and control at any one moment is simply a "part of a 'today.'" The old admonition "Live one day at a time" is wise. It might be even closer to the truth to say, "Live a part of a day at a time." Taken together they are what make a lifetime.

# Metaphor for Life Gym

Frank and Ernest, the notorious cartoon characters, find themselves in the Metaphor for Life Gym. The trainer directs their attention to the exercise equipment and asks, "Which will it be? Running in place or spinning your wheels?"

Often in life it seems these are the only options. For all our efforts, no progress is made. From year to year, nothing changes.

At the start of the New Year, some resolve may well be in order that we see ourselves farther along by year's end. No point to running in place or spinning our wheels. Let's determine that our efforts this year will bring improvement to our lives and those of others.

# Left Alone!

"Left alone!" These words provoke quite different reactions, don't they?

On the one hand, they can mean loneliness. "Left alone!" evokes feelings of isolation and despair and fear.

On the other hand, "Left alone!" can mean rest and quiet. The words can mean a peacefulness we all desire and seek.

In the hectic pace of life, time slips through our grasps as tiny grains of sand through the isthmus of an hourglass. There is so little time to be alone.

Yet, if we neglect solitude, we rob ourselves of the very strength we need to face life's challenges. And we also rob others of the support we could lend them if we were stronger ourselves. To steal away may mean less work, less pleasure, but if we do, it will almost certainly mean more depth, more power.

# What's New?

The year has passed and another has begun. We have said our goodbyes and welcomed the oncoming march of days. Our rituals have marked again the passing of time.

But is there anything new ahead? Or just an endless cycle of days largely filled with routine. Another year little different from those before.

Maybe. But what always portends newness is not simply an unfilled calendar; what portends newness for the days ahead is the spirit we bring to their living. If we launch ahead in a spirit of faith and hope and love, even the routine of passing days will offer us a cherished newness and delight.

# Leaving It Up to Us

An eight-year-old child was once given the assignment to explain God.  He wrote, in part:

One of God's main jobs is making people. He makes them to replace the ones that die, so there will be enough people to take care of things on earth.  He doesn't make grown-ups, just babies. I think because they are smaller and easier to make. That way He doesn't have to take up His valuable time teaching them to talk and walk. He can just leave that to mothers and fathers.

If this eight-year-old is right, it takes more than God to make a person. God leaves a lot to us. Being good mothers and fathers is a very big and important job.

# Born Loser

Brutus P. "Thorny" Thornapple in the comic strip *The Born Loser* converses with himself, saying, ". . . I bowled a 78 tonight . . . . This afternoon, I shot a 212 on the golf course! It's not that I'm bad at sports—I'm just playing the wrong game at the wrong time."

Not only is ability key to success; so is timing. If life seems plagued by failure, maybe the cause is, not a lack of talent or opportunity, but a misapplication of skill to the wrong things at the wrong times.

Want success? Play the right game at the right time.

# Paradise Regained

In 1978, President Bart Giamatti of Yale University issued this memo on his first day in office:

To the members of the University Community:

In order to repair what Milton called the ruin of our grandparents, I wish to announce that henceforth, as a matter of University policy, evil is abolished and paradise is restored.

I trust all of us will do whatever possible to achieve this policy objective.

If only it were so easy to abolish evil. It, of course, is not. But what a better world it would be if we all resolved to deny evil's claim upon life and thwart its purpose. Paradise might not be restored, but, at least, it would be nearer.

# Life's Course

According to Euripides, the Greek tragedian, in *The Trojan Women:*

That mortal is a fool who, prospering, thinks his life has any strong foundation; since our fortune's course of action is the reeling way a madman takes, and no one person is ever happy all the time.

Today, as a result of many modern influences, we think that life should have an ever upward trajectory. We assume that we should be happy all the time and that disappointment or sorrow has no part in mortal life.

But that is a myth. Life's course, as Euripides long ago understood, is not a straight path; it truly is like a madman's way, with periodic stumbles and falls, with all too frequent meanderings, which take us off course.

In the end, maybe, the secret to true happiness in life is not constant happiness, but patient endurance in unhappiness and the skill of recovery.

# Present Mindedness

In *Experience & Education,* the famous American philosopher John Dewey wrote:

> We always live at the time we live and not at some other time, and only by extracting at each present time the full meaning of each present experience are we prepared for doing the same thing in the future. This is the only preparation that in the long run amounts to anything.

Some commentators have argued that Dewey was so immersed in the immediacy of the present moment that he had no interest in the past. Perhaps, it is fairer to say that Dewey understood that the past cannot be changed. The future can, but only if we make the most of our present experience, gleaning from whatever joy or sorrow we currently know the rich lessons of life the present teaches.

These lessons will likely pass us by, however, unless we focus, and, as Dewey rightly suggests, extract their full meaning. That is an assignment to be filled presently.

17

# In the Deep of Night

According to Scripture, God worked most in behalf of the children of Israel, bounded by the Red Sea before and the military might of Pharaoh's army behind, not in the bright light of day, but in the deep dark of night.

So often in life this is how God works. It is when all is dark and God, perhaps, seems most idle that God is busiest in our behalf. Only with the coming light of day is it sometimes clear that for us God has worked "all that night."

In the dark of night, when sometimes all seems lost and our peril certain, let us take heart that God does not sleep. God keeps watch. We may not see until morning's first light: God works even through the night.

# Evil

Mahatma Gandhi, champion of non-violent resistance, believed, according to a 1925 column in *Young India,* the following are evil:

wealth without work
pleasure without conscience
knowledge without character
commerce without morality
science without humanity
worship without sacrifice
politics without principles

At a time when there is much talk about evil, Gandhi's list of evils is a reminder to us in the West of the many forms evil may take, some of which may well be laid at our own feet.

# Walls

Robert Frost was only partly right when he wrote the now famous line in "Mending Wall":

Something there is that doesn't love a wall, . . .

The truth is whatever our real hatred of barriers, we are, nonetheless, experts at their construction. Walls between classes, walls between races, walls between nations, walls between people we like and people we don't like divide the world—all walls of our own making.

But Frost was right in this much: building walls that divide and separate us is contrary to our true nature. Building barriers does not represent us at our best. Deep in the human heart is an unquenchable instinct to hate what divides and separates:

"Something there is that doesn't love a wall,
That wants it down."

And whenever we tear down the walls that divide us, we are truly at our human best.

# The Wrong Side of the Door

Lee Ann Womack has a line in her award-winning tune "I Hope You Dance" that reads:

Whenever one door closes I hope one more opens.

Most of the time we think of doors as only a way out. And so, a closed door is frightening. It means we are trapped, locked in. Our only hope? That another door will open.

But doors are also a way in. The threshold to a new day. Some exciting, even if unknown, tomorrow. Perhaps, the thing we should fear most is not the door that closes, but the door we never open. For in the end, nothing is more tragic than standing on the wrong side of the door and regretting the passage we did not take.

# Of the Stars

The etymologist John Ayto points out that the Latin root of the word *desire* means "of the stars." To have a desire literally means to have some star in view, some glimmering light that appeals to us and attracts us.

Today, there are so many things for us to desire. Many of our desires exceed any delight their fulfillment might produce. Perhaps, this is why we are disappointed again and again.

Maybe, the disappointment would be less and the fulfillment more if we gave our hearts only to the noblest and best, to those things in life that are truly praiseworthy and good, that shine like the stars, that have about them a heavenly glow.

# Doing, Not Just Wishing

How often have you said, "I wish?"

Of course, there are so many things to wish for, and rightly, perhaps. But wishing alone seldom makes them real. If we aren't careful, we all can literally wish our lives away.

Althea M. Bonner offers this sound instruction:

Depart from wishing and do good,
Map out a clean career;
Pursue new paths—they may be rough
But be a pioneer!

Want something wonderful to happen in your life? Well, don't just wish it would occur. Do good, and, maybe, it will.

# A Pencil in God's Hand

In one of her last interviews for a 1989 *Time* magazine article, Mother Teresa, the Roman Catholic Religious Sister who did so much good for the people of India, described herself as "a little pencil in [God's] hand."

What a modest self-appraisal for someone the world believes so great. But, perhaps, her modesty was the very secret of her greatness. Mother Teresa was willing to submit her life to a higher purpose. Who she was and what she did were not merely about her.

Such an attitude may well be the secret to greatness and goodness for us all.

# Shining Faces

"Smiley faces" were once something of a fad and could be found almost anywhere. I hesitate to confess it, but I never really liked the phenomenon. Smiley faces seemed to me too contrived and insincere. I often asked myself if the people who made such use of them really felt and meant the sentiment these symbols were supposed to represent.

And yet, there is nothing more radiant and encouraging than a face bearing a genuine smile. Such a face brightens the world and is reassuring that there is good still at work. A smiling face, aglow from deep within a person, communicates joy and well-being. And truly is a blessed thing.

I can only hope one day to have such a genuine smiling face myself. You, too?

# Hooked

A school of fish, who had played together happily, suddenly noticed one of their members behave strangely. He wouldn't keep up. He disturbed everyone around with his erratic movement through the water. His schoolmates soon were frustrated and wondered why he was behaving so disruptively. No one knew nor could understand.

Only someone outside the group could see. On the bank there was a fisherman with a pole and line. At the end of the line was a hook. The annoying behavior of this one little fish was because he had a hook inside.

As this story from earlier devotional material suggests, the behavior of others is often a mystery to us. We don't know why they are obnoxious or bothersome. Perhaps, like the central character of this fish tale, the strange behavior of those we live with is because they, too, have hooks inside, pulling and tugging from within. Maybe, this is the explanation, and knowing it, we can be more understanding.

# Selective Memory

Someone has said, "The good thing about having a memory is that you can just remember what you want."

How true, really. Our memories, perhaps, are not meant to retain everything, and, maybe, it is best they don't. So much of what happens to us must be left behind if our lives are to go forward. For a canal boat to go through a lock, the gates must close behind before the water can flow in and lift the boat higher.

Selective memory is not a disease of old age; it may well be the clue to good health at any stage of life. We must not forget to forget the past and strive ahead into the future.

# Cheerfully and Gratefully

Once, I received a greeting card thanking me for a gift. It bore these lines of verse by the poet Maya Angelou:

When we give cheerfully
and accept gratefully,
everyone is blessed.

The lines are exactly right. For giving to be complete, it is, not only necessary for the giver to give cheerfully, but also it is necessary for the recipient of the gift to accept gratefully. If either party fails, the true blessedness of the exchange is lost. Perhaps, the greatest expression of gratitude for any gift we receive is to accept it gratefully.

As Portia, in Shakespeare's *Merchant of Venice,* understood, when we give cheerfully and receive gratefully, two people are blessed:

. . . him that gives and him that takes.

# Negative Goodness

Goodness, one devotional writer claims, for a great many people is really a negative thing. What they pride themselves in are the things they don't do. They are very much like the fellow of twenty-one who rather self-righteously judged himself good when he said, "I don't smoke and I don't chew, and I don't go out with girls who do." Many people think themselves good simply because they aren't bad.

But this really is the reverse of true goodness. As the Golden Rule clearly suggests, goodness has more to do with what we do than with what we don't do. This is exactly what makes true goodness such a difficult thing.

It is the person who forgives as he wishes to be forgiven, who helps as she wishes to be helped, who praises as he wishes to be praised that is truly and positively good.

# Pass – Fail

In an installment of the comic strip that bears their names, Frank and Ernest stand before a priest.  Each protests, "I don't want to be a saint or anything -- can I just live life 'pass -- fail'?"

An interesting proposition, no doubt. But think of all that would be lost if this were a common attitude. All that results from our striving to be our best would never be. There would be no invention, no accomplishment, no excellence.

Sure, who wants to be a saint? But who really wants to be anything less than his or her best?

# Optimist or Pessimist?

An article in a wellness magazine asks the question, "Are you an optimist or pessimist?" And it points out the differences between the two for any willing to make a self-diagnosis.

Optimists, on the one hand, feel their actions count. They tend to keep trying. Optimists see alternatives and have a "can do" attitude.

Pessimists, on the other hand, believe that whatever they do doesn't matter. They are easily discouraged and quit. Pessimists see barriers and think things can't be done.

I suppose each of us is one or the other of these, either an optimist or a pessimist. I wonder, though, which of the two is more likely to change the world. And I ask, then, which of the two would I really like to be?

# Responsibility

In an installment of the comic strip *Frank and Ernest,* the following conversation takes place during therapy:

Psychiatrist to patient: "You don't take responsibility for your own actions."

Patient to psychiatrist: "Oh, and whose fault is that?"

Increasingly, this seems to be the way of the world. Everybody's actions are someone else's responsibility. Children blame parents. Citizens blame government. Criminals blame society. No one seems responsible for himself or herself.

But as long as everyone else is responsible, no one is responsible, and nothing gets better. Only when we take responsibility for ourselves is there any hope of a better life—and a better world.

# One Regret

According to André Comte-Sponville in *A Small Treatise on the Great Virtues: The Uses of Philosophy in Everyday Life,* the comedian Woody Allen, best known for his wry self-abasement, making "a spectacle of his fears, failures, and neuroses," reportedly once said, when reflecting upon his life, "The only thing I regret is not being someone else."

To most of us to have only one regret in life would seem the mark of a well-lived life. But for that regret to arise from who one is, or isn't, is sad and tragic. And yet, there are many of us who would make this judgment of our own lives. Never quite satisfied with ourselves, you and I wish we were persons other than who we are.

Who am I? may well be one of life's most important questions. Rather than allow others to answer it for us, we must answer it for ourselves. It is, after all, your question and mine and no one else's to answer.

# Clothes

Each morning when I was a boy, my mother would ask, "What are you wearing to school today?" She was quite clothes conscious.

We live in a culture that presumes, in many ways, that clothes make the person. From the extravagant gowns of Hollywood actresses to the tattered jeans of local teens, what we wear expresses who we are and reveals the groups to which we belong. Whatever the attire, with our clothes, we aim to make a statement.

In the end, of course, it is not what we put on that makes us who we are. It's what's inside. If you really want to make a statement, here is the place to start, with your own views and values, and with who you are, not on the outside, but inside out.

# Tears

There is a moving scene near the end of Rebecca Wells's novel *Divine Secrets of the Ya-Ya Sisterhood.* Sidda gives her mother, with whom she has had a very troubled relationship, a gift.

The gift is a lachrymatory, a tiny jar of tear drops, which Sidda explains, "In olden days . . . was one of the greatest gifts you could give someone. It meant you loved them, that you shared a grief that brought you together."

Some of our relationships seem to provide nothing but grief. Yet, sharing that grief with each other over time may ultimately bring two people together. The struggle of personalities may actually be healing. And in the meantime, bearing that grief may be one of the greatest gifts anyone can give.

# Your Money or Your Life

I have read of two men who strike an odd bargain while incarcerated in a German prison camp during World War II. One agrees to face execution in place of the other if the man who lives transfers all his earthly wealth to the dead man's heirs. The survivor agrees to secure his life, although it means he must for the rest of his days live without his accumulated prosperity.

We think of it as a choice only a few must make at the point of a gun—your money or your life. It is, however, a choice we all must make. What makes for a good life, one really worth living, and what will we give for it? Which would the condemned prisoner's family have preferred—great wealth or him, alive and with them.

Which would you value most—money or life itself?

# Lessons from the Ark

A Minneapolis businessman, in an article for the *Star Tribune,* drew some worthwhile lessons for life from the biblical story of Noah and the ark.

Don't miss the boat, he said. Much of life's successes depends on a keen eye for opportunity. Remember that we are all in the same boat. Life is never really an individual enterprise. Nobody makes it alone. And no matter the storm, remember, there is a rainbow waiting. The going inevitably gets rough from time to time, but seldom does it stay that way. Always be hopeful.

Who would have believed Noah would become a model of business expertise? He was, and is, however, an example of making it through life itself.

# Worry

"Worry," someone has said, "is interest paid on trouble before it is due."

Not a one of us would, of course, pay interest on a loan not yet approved. We recognize that would be foolish. But all of us, sometime or another, will fret over troubles we only imagine and that never happen.

We worry over illnesses we never get and over family, friends, and neighbors, who by and large are able to care for themselves. And, then, when real trouble comes, we are emotionally spent and have none of the resources needed to meet the challenge.

It's all so foolish.

## Don't Belittle

Often, in this highly competitive and frequently bruising world, our first impulse for winning the game of "one-upmanship" is to belittle others. Playground bullies do it. Abusive parents as well. But none of us is immune to the temptation.

To rephrase Kahlil Gibran, "To belittle is to be little." We might think for a moment that we are better than another, stronger or more powerful or more successful, but we aren't. We have only given expression to the littleness in ourselves.

Far bigger is the person who can take the slights of life and the slings of misfortune without recourse to petty retaliation. Bigger is not to belittle.

# Inner Peace

"I think I've found inner peace," a man told his friend. "My therapist told me a way to achieve inner peace is to finish things I start. Today, I finished two bags of potato chips, a lemon pie, and a small box of chocolate. I feel better already."

A way to inner peace may well be to finish things we start. There is, after all, a relief that comes with removing from life any unfinished business. Most of us might be happier if we didn't have long to-do lists. And the only way to eliminate these tasks to be done is to just do them.

But inner peace depends, not only on finishing things we start, but on both starting and finishing the right things. Every little thing is not of equal importance. Start and finish the important ones. That is a more likely way to inner peace.

# Making Peace

The statesman Adlai Stevenson once said, "Making peace is harder than making war," and the lessons of history show he was right.

The word *peace* as used in the Bible never refers merely to the absence of conflict and evil. It refers, instead, always to that condition in which everything needed for the highest good of humankind is present.

There have ever been those who talk wistfully and longingly of peace but never act to improve the conditions upon which peace depends. There will be no peace until we advance the conditions upon which it depends. And that is difficult work. Peace doesn't just happen; it must be made.

# Keeping Peace

The Chinese, unlike us, have three words in their vocabulary for peace. One of the words is formed by two signs. One of the signs means heart. The other sign, composed of two parallel lines, stands for two. The idea: when two hearts are level, the necessary conditions for peace are met.

Nowhere is peace more difficult to keep, perhaps, than in relationships with others—friends, co-workers, business associates, group members. And, maybe, it is because the very conditions the Chinese recognize as necessary for peace seldom exist, and even when they do, are difficult to maintain: a fundamental sense of equality and mutuality, the kind of level plane between hearts united in partnership by a common respect and regard.

Want peace? Work for partnership.

# Lasting Peace

In his poem "Christmas:1924," Thomas Hardy observed:

"PEACE upon earth!" was said, We sing it,
And pay a million priests to bring it.
After two thousand years of mass
We've got as far as poison-gas.

Ah, Mr. Hardy, we have gotten even further—to atom bombs and hollow point bullets, to napalm and assault rifles, to lethal injections and drive-by shootings. Look how far we've come. Is peace any more than a dream?

Yes, if we do our parts. Always the worst requires our best. Our highest and noblest dreams guide us in the right and ennoble our lives. In the worst of times, peace is our guiding star, and it can be our common cause.

# Someplace

The protagonist of the cartoon series *B.C.* mused to himself:

You can be early, or you can be late,
Show up beforehand or make people wait,
You can hide in a mine, or find mountains to climb,
But you gots to be someplace all of the time.

Time and place are realities we cannot escape. We spend much of life longing for the past or dreaming about the future and wishing we were somewhere else. No doubt, we all know or can imagine better times and places than now and here.

But the real challenge we all face is to make the most of life here and now. Because we "gots to be someplace all of the time."

# One More Thing

In the days of our ancestors, men and women were willing to give thanks for very little. Very little seems to have been all they expected. Decent shelter, simple clothing, adequate food. Not much more. But, nonetheless, our forebears seemed warmly appreciative for what they had, grateful for any kindness or benefit.

Now, of course, it is very different. Nothing short of the most extravagant gifts seems enough to us. If we can't get a new smartphone, an expensive wardrobe, a new car or house, a big bonus, we feel deprived. It appears the more we want, the less thankful we are for what we have.

Actually, its origin is unknown. It is a monk's prayer: "You have given so much to us. Give us one more thing: a grateful heart."

So, let our prayer be to receive grateful hearts for things great and small.

# Home

*Home.* No word in the English language, I suppose, is sweeter than this. The word for most of us elicits precious memories, and even for those whose memories of home are less than happy, it is a word that evokes a deep longing to have a home, to find a home.

But home is never just a place. In some conditions, it is, of course, easier to make a home than it is in others. Want and need may increase the challenge and difficulty of making a place a home. But even in the worst of circumstances, honesty and industry can persevere in making a home.

For in the end, people makes places what they are. We all need places where people know our names, and we feel we matter. Where people care for us for our sakes. And we all can make places like that.

# Too Many Notes

A jazz musician was once asked about the secret of his music. He replied, "I play no more notes than necessary."

Too much of life is overfilled. Perhaps, there would be greater rhythm and more beauty if we could eliminate the superfluous and concentrate on the necessary. One of Mozart's critics once complained about his music that there were simply too many notes.

Maybe, that's the case with your life. For a change, why not try playing no more notes than necessary, and look for the difference! You might find the music of your life much more harmonious and beautiful.

# Spring

It's an old Irish blessing:

May soft be the grass you walk on,
May fair be the skies above you,
May true be the joys that surround you,
May dear be the hearts that love you.

Spring is a time of rediscovery, of coming to know again the simple beauties and joys of life: green grass and fair skies and simple pleasures and the love of dear hearts.

These spring days stop, look, listen. Let life begin in you all over again.

# Negative Capability

An installment of the comic strip *The Family Circus* pictures parents dragging their children into church loudly protesting, "But we don't want to learn about heaven; we want it to be a surprise!"

Well, here is the dilemma of religious life. Is religious life primarily a matter of learning, of gaining knowledge, of being well-informed, through much study and thought? Or is religious life primarily a matter of being affected strongly, filled with wonder and astonishment, of, yes, being surprised again and again by the awesome and illusive power and presence of the Divine?

The truth, of course, is that religious life is something of both in the right balance and proper relationship. A matter of heart and mind, thought and feeling. Someone has said faith is a "negative capability": it is a way of facing uncertainties and doubt without resort to knowledge or feeling alone. It is a way of embracing life's mysteries with heart and mind.

# Rich

According to an old Chinese proverb found in the *Tao Te Ching,* "He who knows he has enough is rich."

The wisdom of this proverb is largely lost on us today. In today's sophisticated and affluent society, the list of our needs and wants is almost endless, and it never seems that we have enough of anything.

In fact, the more we have, the more we think we need and want of the vast array of gadgets and gizmos that we now take to be outward symbols of true wealth. The vicious cycle of buying and spending begins in a vain attempt to acquire enough things to enhance self-esteem and establish a certain status.

The old Chinese proverb has it right. When we find contentment in life's essentials, we are delivered from the terrible tyranny of things. And, indeed, we are rich.

# Spring Thoughts

Alfred, Lord Tennyson's line in "Locksley Hall" easily comes to mind this time of year:

> In the spring a young man's fancy lightly turns
> to thoughts of love.

Somehow, warm days and bright skies make us feel more alive and favorable toward others. The transformation seems part of the ritual of spring. But wouldn't life be better all around if we let spring thoughts pervade the whole year? If kindness prevailed throughout the year, maybe, the cold of winter and the heat of summer would be less oppressive.

This spring, perhaps, we should resolve to allow what occurs naturally this time of year, not only to have its beginning, but also to have longevity. Maybe then, all year our hearts would be full of spring.

# What's Left Behind

In "Ode: Intimations of Immortality," the poet William Wordsworth has this guidance for all who wish to move forward in life:

> Though nothing can bring back the hour
> Of splendor in the grass, of glory in the flower;
> We will grieve not, rather find
> Strength in what remains behind; . . .

I can think of no better motto for advancing into the future. The past is now behind. We can grieve over what has been lost. Or we can let our memories be a source of strength, inspiring us to better and brighter days ahead.

No doubt, the best way to honor the past is to work for tomorrow.

# Courage to Be

Among Shakespeare's most famous lines is the one from *Hamlet* that reads:

To be, or not to be: that is the question: . . .

One of life's greatest challenges is to decide who we are in the face of all those forces that would determine our identities. Circumstances may well set limits to self-determination, but they are not irresistible and need not be decisive. We may refuse to allow them solely to define us. Somewhere within, there is courage to be drawn upon in defining the terms of our existence and who we will be.

The question is whether we will summon that courage and exert ourselves against the conditions of birth and the present circumstances of life to be our best selves.

# Listening for a Song

Once, while in a card shop, I found a very special get-well card. It was a miniature, battery-operated keyboard with music to several popular tunes like "Singin' in the Rain" and "I'm Looking Over a Four Leaf Clover."

Quickly, I decided to try "Somewhere Over the Rainbow." In playing the notes, I thought of the lyrics, which describe a place or moment in time "where the clouds are far behind" and "troubles melt like lemon drops."

And that's when I realized, even in the deepest of troubles, there is a song, if only we listen.

# Family Feuds

According to *Wikipedia,* a feud is a long-running argument between people that begins, rightly or wrongly, because one person believes he or she has been harmed. The continual cycle of resentment and revenge that often ensues makes restoration of harmonious relationships difficult.

Feuds are facts of family life. They can last decades, and very often not even in death is there reconciliation. No family is immune. These fractures in family relationships represent a grave tragedy.

Can family feuds be healed? According to one writer, there are a few strategies to try:

Do something right away: don't count on time.
Face the facts: what divides must be taken seriously.
And don't expect miracles: it takes two to reconcile.
It takes hard work: but work can pay off.

# An Attitude of Gratitude

A researcher on stress claims that two attitudes largely affect the quality of everyday life. One is revenge. It is the most destructive.

The other is gratitude. Dr. Hans Selye of McGill University argues, "Among all the emotions, [this] is one which more than any other accounts for the presence or absence of stress in human relations: . . ."

Want contentment and peace of mind? Be grateful. Life may not be all you'd like. But being thankful might just make the difference in how you see your life and as a result how you live it.

# Letting Go

A fable attributed first to Epictetus and later to Aesop tells of a boy who put his hand into a pitcher containing figs and hazelnuts. Quite greedily he clutched as many as his hand could hold. But when he tried to remove his fist, he found the narrow neck of the container prevented him. The boy cried in misery. An astute observer nearby pointed out to him that the secret was to let go a little.

Often, we make ourselves unhappy simply because we won't let go. We won't let go of our opinions or our grievances or our prejudices. But that's exactly what is needed if we are to move ahead and know joy.

The children's poet Shel Silverstein makes the point this way:

> Our anchor's too big for our ship,
> . . . So we're sittin' here tryin' to think.
> If we leave it behind we'll be lost.
> If we haul it on board, we will sink.
> If we sit and keep talkin' about it,
> It will soon be too late for our trip.
> It sure can be rough on a sailor
> When the anchor's too big for the ship.

Maybe, it's time to let go.

# Rarely Happy

People, it seems, are rarely happy with what they have, no matter how much or how little. "By much of the world's standards, even minimum-wage U.S. workers," someone has written, "are wealthy beyond hope [of much of the world], yet they do not feel rich."

There are many reasons to improve the wages of people in this country and around the world, particularly the pay of those at the lowest ranks of compensation. But, perhaps, the real cause of unhappiness in modern life lies deeper. We have forgotten how to be happy.

The secret to true wealth is the same for all. It's gratitude. No one who is thankful can really feel impoverished or unhappy.

# Meaning

John Gardner, the respected leader, activist, author, and reformer writes:

Meaning is not something you stumble across, like the answer to a riddle or the prize in a treasure hunt. Meaning is something you build into your life. You build it out of your own past, out of your affections and loyalties, out of the experience of humankind as it is passed on to you, out of your own talent and understanding, out of the things you believe in, out of the things and people you love, out of the values for which you are willing to sacrifice something. The ingredients are there. You are the only one who can put them together into that unique pattern that will be your life. Let it be a life that has dignity and meaning for you. If it does, then the particular balance of success or failure is of less account.

We often think that the meaning of life is something to be found. Wrong. It is something to be made. And that's our work. Yours and mine.

# Perennial B.C.

The following conversation transpires in the comic strip *B.C.*:

"Man, the Bible is a tough book. I mean, what could be worse than the fall of Adam and Eve?"

"The winter of Adam and Eve?"

Even if humorous, this exchange illustrates the human condition. How often in time of trouble, personal or national, do we expect the resources of faith to provide answers? But we, like the cave dwellers of *B.C.*, have made no advance preparation. We are generally ignorant of the faith we hope will now be our salvation.

If faith is to be a refuge and strength in time of trouble, advance preparation is required.

# No Immunity

Dennis the Menace represents us all when once at bedtime he prayed, "If I can have immunity, here's what I did today."

Like Dennis, we all want mercy. We would like to think that we can be spared the repercussions of our conduct. Unfortunately, not even the greatest mercy of all can give us immunity. Long after we are forgiven, we still must live with the consequences of our failures.

Far better that we first think of the consequences of our deeds rather than live with them forever after. For in the end, there may be forgiveness, but there is no immunity.

# Hope Eternal

Between 1937 and 1949, Stalin deported millions of ethnic minorities to special settlements in the USSR. According to an unsubstantiated report, he ordered thirty thousand Germans living in Russia to be loaded onto cattle cars and transported into the wilderness. They left with nothing to survive the winter but the clothes they wore.

As they disembarked, contemplating their plight, they began to sing an ancient hymn. Reportedly, of the thirty thousand deported, only twelve thousand survived to see spring.

The loss and sorrow was, no doubt, great. But all was not lost. Again and again, for those who hope, triumph is possible. And spring comes. This is the great truth of Easter, not only that hope is eternal, but that hope also triumphs.

# Lookin' in All the Wrong Places

Even now, after two thousand years of instruction and celebration, the claim of Jesus's resurrection stretches the limits of belief. Maybe, the difficulty lies in the focus of our search for convincing evidence. Too often, we look, as did the first disciples who went to the tomb Easter morning, in all the wrong places. The question posed to the women long ago may apply equally to us, "Why do you look for the living among the dead?"

The true evidence of Jesus's resurrection is to be found, as the question implies, in the course of daily living. The risen Christ meets us in the very toils, conflicts, sufferings, joys, and triumphs of life as an abiding presence with us. As the famous scholar Albert Schweitzer claimed, the evidence of Jesus's resurrection is found in the here and now.

Jesus said, "I am with you always, to the end of the age." Daily sheltered by gracious powers, we know he lives and is with us.

# Truce

Finally, after more than a century, pen and ink, not a shotgun and bullets, sealed the end of one of the country's longest running feuds. In 2003, newspapers reported that descendants of the Hatfield and McCoy families gathered to sign a truce, bringing their long-standing feud, which claimed at least a dozen lives, to an end.

The conflict is believed to have started with the murder of a McCoy. Relations worsened during a dispute over a pig. The battle escalated when a violent confrontation resulted in the death of a Hatfield and the murder of three McCoys. In an attempt to settle matters, a group of Hatfields attacked a McCoy family in what became known as the 1888 New Year's Night Massacre.

Finally, hostility decreased, and the families receded into obscurity. In signing the truce, representatives of the Hatfields and McCoys said, "We ask . . . that we be forever remembered as those that bound together the hearts of two families . . . ."

Even when the conflict is long and hard, harmony is still possible for those who set their hearts and minds on peace.

# Good Times

Dennis the Menace, in an episode of the well-known cartoon strip, asks his elderly grandfather, "How come the days have to be **old** to be **good**?"

Despite what we at times think, the days don't have to be old to be good. Just as days of old were often good, so likely will be the days ahead. Some days will be good and some days will be bad. A lot depends on us.

But, no doubt, the good days of life are not behind; they are yet ahead, especially if we make them so.

# Complain, Complain, Complain

One humorist has said that of all the theories experts have developed to explain the origin of language, the best is the one that maintains that language was born out of the deep-seated, human need to complain.

A casual observer might well agree. Listen to human conversation, and it soon appears many of us use words to no higher end. We rant and rave about the things, the people, and the circumstances we don't like.

In an episode of *The Family Circus*, it's the end of the day. Seven-year-old Billy is on his way to bed, his shaggy dog, Sam, trailing behind. He says, "I can't think of anything to complain about, so I must have had a good day."

Most days, most of us could say the same.

# Present Tense

In school, we all learned that verbs have three principle tenses—present, past, and future. So, too, does life itself.

The fact is, even if only unconsciously, each of us chooses one of these tenses in which to live. Many of us live our lives in the past, caught up with what was. Some of us live our lives in the future, preoccupied with what will or might be.

Too few of us live life consistently in the present tense. And so, we miss much that is right now, right here. Memory and hope are certainly a part of what makes us distinctively human. But the best time of life is now, and we should live most of life in the present tense.

# How to Disagree

No matter how long they have known each other and no matter how close they may have become, friends still disagree. A mark of true friendship is that people learn to appreciate their differences and do not allow them to spoil their relationship.

Two old friends are reported to have traveled together often. Once commenting on the relationship, one said in effect:

We discussed everything you can think of. We agreed on the great things. We did not always agree on other things. It was a good arrangement, because while we agreed enough to be congenial, we differed enough to make it interesting.

It would be a dull world, indeed, if we all thought alike. The secret to disagreement is not to give little things more importance than they deserve. And in the end, is there really any subject important enough to let it rob us of a friendship? Maybe. But such subjects must be very few.

# Reflection

The Quaker poet Bernard Barton somewhere writes:

As I walked by myself, I talked to myself
And myself replied to me;
And the questions myself then put to myself
With their answers, I give to thee.

With the busy pace of life today, there is hardly time anymore to reflect. And there is little incentive provided by modern culture to inspire us to think. Perhaps, this is one of the losses in a society that places such high priority on mere entertainment.

Nonetheless, we all want answers. Often, the answers we seek are waiting inside our very selves. We will never find them, however, unless we take time to think and reflect and, yes, talk to ourselves.

# To Die For

All of us die, eventually, *of* something: disease, an accident, old age. This is the end result sooner or later. And in a sense, all of life between the first breath and the last is but a waiting to die of something.

In the meantime, however, if life is truly to be meaningful, we must find something we are willing to die *for.* Something noble and worthwhile.

Perhaps, these are the choices. If we all must die, will it be to die of something or to die for something? Of course, few of us will ever be obliged literally to make this choice. But in a real sense, don't we all figuratively have to decide whether we will die of something or die for something? Will we idle by, cautiously, without risk or endangerment? Or will we venture ourselves, our lives and fortunes, in the cause of something great? Perhaps, this choice, more than any other, determines whether we ever really live.

# Stuck!

Remember that horrible scene some years ago of a little girl who had fallen into a well pipe no more than a foot in diameter? Utterly helpless, she was stuck between air and light above and darkness and certain death below. Little Jessica was suspended for more than a day between the promise of rescue and its actual fulfillment.

Often in life we find ourselves in similar spots, stuck between promise and fulfillment. We are like Matthew Arnold's "foil'd circuitous wanderer":

> Wandering between two worlds, one dead,
> The other powerless to be born, . . .

All we can do is hold fast and firm. Our only assurance is that patient plodding in time shows results.

# Nothing

Imagine the worst thing that can happen. We are, of course, immediately inclined to think of some misfortune or disaster.

But sometimes, the worst thing that can happen is nothing. Why? Because when nothing happens, everything remains the same. There is not as much as the potential for good to occur.

In the end, only nothing comes from nothing. That's a fate we must all avoid.

# Choosing What Matters

Sue Monk Kid in *The Secret Life of Bees,* puts a finger on the source of much of our trouble as human beings.

In the story, a disagreement ensues after May, a pivotal character in the book, paints her house pink. Most of the town thinks it it's the tackiest color they have ever seen, but May says it lifts her heart. Finally, one of May's friends laughs and says:

"You know, some things, don't matter that much, . . .Like the color of a house. How big is that in the overall scheme of life? . . . The whole problem with people is—"

"They don't know what matters and what doesn't," another friend interjects.

"I was gonna say," the friend continues, "The problem is they *know* what matters, but they don't *choose* it. . . . The hardest thing on earth is choosing what matters."

Much of life's trouble results from our failure to choose what matters. Trouble we would not have to bear if we considered things in the overall scheme of life and gave our attention to what really matters. Why don't we?

# For All Lands

In the fray of life, we often forget, just as we have hopes and dreams, others also do. In lands afar, just as here at home, hearts are beating with similar aspirations for justice and peace.

It is easy to believe that our land is the best, our skies so blue, the sun so bright, and to forget that everywhere the skies are as blue as ours and the sun as bright.

As Lloyd Stone in his poem "This Is My Song" suggests, knowing hearts everywhere have longings as true and high as ours, ours should be a song of peace for all lands as well as for our own.

# Blackballed

In the syndicated comic strip *The Family Circus,* an implied bedtime conversation takes place between mother and child. Mom, pointing her finger to an angry-faced child, says:

"Yes, you have to include her. You can't blackball your sister from your prayers."

How often, hands folded, knees bent—at least, figuratively—we pray for ourselves and those like us, consciously or unconsciously omitting much of the human family, especially those unlike us and particularly those we simply don't like.

I wonder, does God hear such prayers from which we have blackballed others? Perhaps, God does. But I still wonder, how is God disposed to answer such prayers? It might be wise for us all to wonder.

# Differences

Black/White
Rich/Poor
Fat/Trim
Pretty/Ugly
Smart/Slow
Democrat/Republican
Male/Female
Differences

Although we are of a common biological species, more like each other than we are like any other creature on the face of the earth, we human beings seem to take unusual interest and great pride in distinguishing ourselves from one another.

Certainly, there can be no denying that differences do, in fact, exist among us, some of them quite obvious, others of them very subtle.

But just imagine what a better world it would be if we focused, not on our differences, but on what we have in common. Because our differences need not divide us, unless we insist they do. They are only superficial and finally trivial.

# All Suffer

In his famous play *The Persians,* the ancient Greek dramatist Aeschylus invited his audience to contemplate the Battle of Salamis at which the Persians had defeated the Greeks. Aeschylus's aim was to have the Greeks think of their defeat from their enemies' point of view. It was a clear risk: a similar attempt only years before by another Greek playwright had resulted in a riot.

But this time, the reaction was different. The audience wept for their dead enemies. Only four years earlier, the Persians had destroyed the magnificent cities of the Greeks. Aeschylus succeeded in portraying the terrible suffering of all humankind, friend and foe alike, in a way that inspired sympathy and defeated hatred in the hearts of his fellow citizens.

Perhaps, even today, some recognition that we all suffer, quite often at each other's hands, would cause us to hurt each other less often.

# Nature's Art

They are among nature's most beautiful displays. And they remind us of the beauty that over and around us always lies. They are sunrises and sunsets.

The magnificence of these displays throughout winter, spring, summer, and fall are nature's art. Can any of us behold their beauty and not, if only tentatively, conclude that there is a goodness at the center of things? And that it surrounds us every day, no matter what happens between morning and night?

Sunrises and sunsets—subtle hints of such a claim? Maybe. Nonetheless, a reassuring thought.

# Grace

A well-known painting by Norman Rockwell portrays a mother and son, heads bowed, giving thanks before eating in a crowded restaurant. Two bystanders look on in bemusement.

In many ways, here is a portrait of our time. In an age where most of us think that whatever we have is the result of our own efforts, any expression of gratitude to unseen powers is met with skepticism.

Most of us, even if we would not admit it, tend to think that we have worked for and earned the things we have. Clearly, in addition to all we have received, one thing is still missing—a sense of grace.

# Give Me!

The central figure in a comic strip tells his mom that he figures God must get tired of hearing the same old prayers, so he decided at bedtime to recite "Humpty Dumpty."

I think God must get tired of hearing the same old prayers from us, particularly since most of the time what we say is "Give me!" Even a child's rhyme might be a relief to God's ears.

Is God nothing more than a celestial Santa Claus with nothing to do but give us what we want? Most of us would not accept this idea, but who could tell from the content of most of our prayers?

# No Difference

Once, a candidate for the Democratic Party's nomination for the presidency withdrew from the race because of a low rating in the polls. Following her announcement, a major news network conducted a survey, asking people if they believed the candidate's withdrawal would make a difference in the race. Some 91 percent of respondents answered negatively; only 9 percent responded affirmatively.

They are questions we might all ask: Were I to disappear from the scene, what would family, friends, coworkers say? Does my presence make a difference in the quality of their lives, perhaps, even more, in the outcome of things?

Would we not all hope to get something better than a 9 percent favorable response? Perhaps, it isn't praise or love or fame that matters most in life, but the transforming effect we have on others.

# Ignorant

It's not just the stuff of which cartoons are made.

Someone asks, "Why are you so ignorant?"

The party of the inquiry responds, "I don't know!"

Yes, it's the stuff of life itself. How often we plead ignorance and when questioned blame our ignorance on our ignorance. In the end, the party responsible for what you know and when you know it is you. Why? Because no one else can know for you.

Even in the age of information, only we can overcome our own ignorance.

# Choices

A popular song of the past asks us:

> Did you ever have to make up your mind?
> Pick up on one and leave the other behind
> It's not often easy, and not often kind
> Did you ever have to make up your mind?

Of course, we all have, and it is not often easy. Perhaps, because which alternative to choose is seldom clear. Most choices are draws, no one option much better than the other.

But still we must choose. It may, in the end, be less important that we select the best option than it is to make the best of the option we choose. And so, once we have made up our minds, give our all to the best outcome.

# Meeting the Night

It often seems that there is so little light for all the things that must be done in a day that night strikes us as wasted time. But night has its own important place in life.

An old prayer says:

O Lord God,
Who has given us the night for rest,
I pray that in my sleep
My soul may remain awake to You,
Steadfastly adhering to Your love.
As I lay aside my cares to relax
And relieve my mind,
May I not forget Your infinite
And unresting care for me.
And in the way,
Let my conscience be at peace,
So that when I rise tomorrow,
I am refreshed in body, mind and soul.

As the prayer gently suggests, how we meet the day is very much determined by how we meet the night.

# Friends

One of the most popular television series of all time was *Friends*.

The series, which will run indefinitely in syndication, is a reminder just how important friends are to a well-lived life. They are, as the ancient writer Sirach put it, "a life-saving medicine."

The series also points out just how hard it is to make and keep friends these days. Life has become so hectic and often relations so strained that giving to relationships the time and effort they require must be intentional.

Ralph Waldo Emerson had it right, to have a friend you must be a friend. How odd that a TV comedy is required to remind us of this great truth.

# Perfect

A couple decided to set a date to marry. They concluded that their engagement had certainly proved that neither of the two is perfect.

On the basis of their experience, they also concluded that something else is true. Although neither of them is perfect, they are perfect for each other.

No relationship is ideal, because no two people are perfect. The great challenge in any marriage is to find the good that exists between two people given each other's faults and failures. And that is a good a couple must work toward by embracing each other's imperfections.

# Getting a Grip

In a cartoon strip that bears his name, Frank confesses a sentiment we all feel from time to time. He complains to Ernest:

"Just when I finally got a grip on things, the handle fell off."

Life in its many forms—work, family, health, and friendships—doesn't always conform to our wills. It has an almost perverse way of getting out of hand.

The secret to overcoming life's difficulties, however, may, not so much be getting a grip on things, but on ourselves, determining our attitudes and reactions to the many things that befall us against our wills. Maybe, we are the ones, the only ones, in fact, we can get a grip on.

# Sleep

Sleep is a precarious state of being in which we move in and out of awareness. It seems only natural that as children we would fear and resist a condition from which we have not had enough experience to know if we will recover. But as adults, we need not fear sleep.

There is a nighttime prayer that reads:

> I am going now into the sleep,
> Be it that I in health shall wake;
> If death be to me in deathly sleep,
> Be it that in thine own arm's keep,
> O God of grace, to new life I wake;
> O be it in thy dear arm's keep,
> O God of grace, that I shall awake!

If in such faith we can come to sleep, then the darkness truly can do us no harm.

# Easy Living

A once popular song celebrates summer, describing it as a time of easy living.

Living is almost never easy. We wish it were. A life without difficulty and disappointment seems hardly more than something to sing about, a fantasy hardly ever fulfilled.

Yet, although we aren't inclined to think so, maybe, life isn't meant to be easy. It might be rather dull if it was, and without the challenges difficulty and disappointment offer, perhaps, we would never become better selves.

It could be that hard knocks make for better lives than does easy living.

# Away This Hate

In his country hit "I Hate Everything," George Strait describes the man who hates everything. He hates his job. He hates his life. If it weren't for the kids, he'd hate his ex-wife. He hates summer, winter, fall and spring, red and yellow, purple, blue and green. He hates everything.

Someone has said that the worst of the present day is that men and women hate one another so damnably. Indeed, the world seems everywhere divided between parties hostile and opposed to each other: nation against nation, tribe against tribe, party against party, individual against individual.

In *Antony and Cleopatra,* Shakespeare may well have identified the cause long ago when he wrote:

In time we hate that which we often fear.

Maybe, we would hate less if we aimed to understand what we fear. Who really wants to be the person who hates everything?

# Joyful Calm

In *The Lotus-Eaters,* Alfred, Lord Tennyson, quoting "what the inner spirit sings," wrote:

'There is no joy but calm!'

He understood that calm is essential to health and well-being.

More and more, we seem to prefer haste and hurry, busyness and excitement, only to find our lives less joyful.

Perhaps, we must work at calm. And some do. They take up meditation. They travel to remote places. They undergo therapy. All worthwhile.

But not entirely necessary if we make for ourselves places of quiet repose within the daily routine and create for ourselves moments of joyful calm.

# Make Life Worthwhile

These days it seems the chorus sung around us is increasingly off-key. The blend of voices is more and more sharp and shrill. Ever ask why we, among the most blessed of the world, should find so much to gripe and groan about?

A poet once wrote:

> May every soul that touches mine—
> Be it the slightest contact—
> Get there from some good;
> Some little grace; one kindly thought;
> One aspiration yet unfelt;
> One bit of courage
> For the darkening sky;
> One gleam of faith
> To brave the thickening ills of life;
> One glimpse of brighter skies
> Beyond the gathering mists—
> To make this life worth while; . . .

If the point of living is to make life worthwhile, if that is your purpose and mine, what on earth do we think is gained by all our criticism and complaint? Wouldn't it be better if we made our voices harmonious and pleasing? Wouldn't a "little grace," a "kindly thought," a "bit of courage," a "gleam of faith" more likely make this life worthwhile for others and ultimately for ourselves, too?

# Summertime

Summer is short.  Winter often lingers into spring and eagerly returns in the fall, leaving too few days of warm sunshine and refreshing showers. As a result, nature is left with little time to flourish.  Shrubs and flowers can waste none of summer if they are to grow and blossom.

Often, the biblical writers compare life itself to the flowers and grasses of summer. They start up, mature, and quickly fade. In this respect, they are apt symbols of life as we know it. Time here is brief.

If you and I are to make our best showings, we must be busy. There is little of life's summer. We must grow and blossom while the sun shines and the refreshing rains fall.

# Talk to Me

Dennis the Menace tells his friend, "I like talking to myself, Joey, 'cause I always get the answers I like."

Some psychologists tell us that we all talk to ourselves, and we do it almost unknowingly. In our minds, voices from our pasts are constantly running, and these voices shape our notions of who we are and what life is like, whether good or evil. In fact, some psychologists maintain that if we want good mental health, we must identify these voices, interrupt them, and talk to ourselves in healthier ways.

Dennis is right, then. We do talk to ourselves. What we often need to do is stop the old, debilitating voices and strike up brand new conversations with ourselves.

# Make Some Mistakes

In an episode of the cartoon strip *The Family Circus*, an older brother instructs his younger sibling with these words:

"You can learn from your mistakes, so be sure to make some."

The older brother, no doubt, has often heard his parents exhort him to learn from his mistakes, and obviously, he has made some. But even if the lesson is somehow misapplied to his younger brother, it bears an important truth for all ages.

Not only do we make mistakes—that is inevitable—and not only should we learn from them, but we should never be so cautious or afraid not to risk failure and wrong. Perhaps, we should be sure to make some mistakes; they often are life's best teachers.

# The Weather Inside

A popular tune warns, "The weather outside is frightful." That certainly can be the case.

But no matter the conditions outdoors, life beckons us all to make the weather inside warm and welcoming. And that is a matter of genuine hospitality.

Make home, no matter how humble or grand, a place of graciousness and acceptance, and so a loving and lovely place, in which all who come will say, "The weather inside is delightful."

# Whose Good?

That famous cartoon kid Dennis the Menace finds himself in time-out, obviously incarcerated for some misbehavior. He laments, "I still don't understand HOW this is for my own good."

From early age we are instructed to believe that any restraint upon our misbehavior is somehow for our own good. Seldom, of course, do we really believe that. But imagine what our lives would be like if there were never any limits placed upon our behavior, and, worse, what we as persons would be.

It never is immediately clear how reprimand or restraint is for our own good. But boundaries, carefully imposed and respectfully observed, make us, not only disciplined, but truly free.

# My Way

The two principal characters in the cartoon strip *The Born Loser* are engaged in a serious disagreement.

"We're going to do this my way!" one declares.

"No! We're going to do it my way!" the other responds adamantly.

"Arguing like this is silly, Gladys! Can't we agree to a compromise?"

To which Gladys answers, "Very well. . . . We're not going to do it your way!"

We may idolize figures who, like Frank Sinatra, say, "I did it my way." We may wish somehow to do the same, but such a strategy leads only to what the Greeks called Pyrrhic victories—triumphs not worth the costs.

Unfortunately, Gladys fails to understand that she may do things her way, but in so doing, she loses the more blessed opportunity of collaboration. Many of us make the same mistake.

# The Prolonged Goodbye

Shakespeare's Juliet was right when she said:

... parting is such sweet sorrow, ...

For in every goodbye there is a mixture of delight and sadness.

All of life is something of a prolonged goodbye. We must say goodbye to the innocence of childhood. We must say goodbye to the frivolities of youth. In time we must say goodbye to family and friends. And in the end, of course, we must say goodbye to vitality and life itself.

The "sweet sorrow" of goodbye is integral to all of life. For that reason we should become expert at farewells. Knowing when to hold on and when to let go is a true virtue. For the better we are at goodbyes, the better we are at life itself.

# Everyone's Struggle

Rubin "Hurricane" Carter, the well-known boxer, was convicted of a crime, which a preponderance of the evidence at the time clearly indicated he did not commit. He was sentenced for murder to three life terms in prison while still a very young man. In prison he wrote his life's story, which attracted the attention of a New York youth and three Canadians who tirelessly worked for Carter's release, succeeding in the end. By that time Carter had spent more than twenty years in a New Jersey prison.

In the course of his long imprisonment, Carter determined to fight. Knowing he might not ever win release, he disciplined himself never to be incarcerated in spirit. Through education, reflection, and training, he prevailed against the harsh realities of prison life to become a man truly free at the deepest levels of the human soul.

He once said that we must all transcend what aims to hold us. There are many forces at work in human life that without resistance entrap and imprison us: background, prejudice, ability, opportunity. Add to that list past failure. But true freedom is never merely a matter of external factors. Freedom is an attitude and orientation of the self. It comes only to those who transcend what aims to hold them. And in this respect, freedom is everyone's struggle.

# Stick-to-itiveness

A television ad features a somewhat overweight figure working out at the gym. He weighs himself, then makes one lap around the equipment, and then weighs himself again, only to discover that his limited effort has made no difference in his weight.

Psychologists have named this disposition immediate gratification. These days, we want instant results. But any important accomplishment takes time and persistence on our parts.

Success is time-consuming. Marriage is. Friendship is. Community is. Every truly good thing is. And we only fool ourselves to think otherwise.

# What's Good for Me?

In a comic strip, Frank makes the following admission to Earnest:

"I'm figuring out what's good for me, but only by the process of elimination."

Figuring out what's good for anyone may well be one of life's greatest challenges. In his translation of Juvenal's "Tenth Satire," the poet John Dryden states the issue emphatically:

Look round the habitable world, how few
Know their own good, or knowing it, pursue.

It may well be clear that some things are not good for anybody. But whether most things are good for you or me really cannot be decided in advance. We have to figure it all out—largely by a process of elimination. In many things good may actually be a matter of experiment. Only with trial, which sometimes meets with success and sometimes meets with failure, do we actually come to know what's good for you or me.

# Forgiveness Denied

Perhaps, one of the most tragic figures in all of literature is Stavrogin, the protagonist in Dostoevsky's novel *Demons*. Stavrogin has been harmed by one of his fellows. He is not opposed to forgiveness, but he makes it so greatly demanding that it is virtually unattainable.

Stavrogin represents an evil that too often exists in many of us. Few are those who say that they can not or will not forgive. But there are those of us, like Stavrogin, who establish such stringent requirements for forgiveness that no offender could possibly meet them.

And that is tragic, robbing life of much of its goodness, filling our souls with anger and resentment, making life more fractured and unhappy than it truly need be. An unreadiness to forgive is, as Dostoevsky's novel suggests, a real and destructive evil.

# No!

**no**[1] (nō), *adv., adj., n., pl.* **noes, nos,** v. *—adv.* **1.** (a negative used to express dissent, denial, or refusal, as in response to a question or request)

It's clear from Webster's definition exactly what makes it the most hated word in the English language. Nobody likes to be told no, especially today, in the age of freedom and independence and personal autonomy. No is regarded as an infringement and an insult. After all, what right does anyone have to refuse or deny?

In *Newsweek,* this little, pesky word was actually the subject of a feature article. A number of experts consulted by the authors of the article clearly argued that such disdain for the word is a serious threat to virtue and common good. Acceptance of inescapable limits, the ability and necessity to work with others, and sacrifice in the interest of long-term greater goods are all at risk. If they are right, then no is really not a bad word.

# Life Story

Day by day each of us writes a life story. Circumstances provide the background. Events of the day make up the plot. Others in our lives constitute the cast of characters.

But the quality of the stories themselves, we largely determine. The famous French philosopher Paul Ricoeur is credited with saying that all life has a narrative shape, and our calling as human beings is to live a life worth recounting.

In the end, every person is an author. The stories of our lives are written as we go. What author wouldn't like to have to his or her credit a story worth recounting—again and again and again?

# Whose Job Is It?

Those young inquiring minds of the comic strip *The Family Circus* ask a question provoked, no doubt, by their exposure to all those televised home improvement shows:

"Instead of cleaning our rooms, couldn't we have a decorator give them a makeover?"

Programs portraying free makeovers, of course, have their appeal; but, in many ways, just as these hopeful cartoon characters unsuspectingly betray, they are also misleading. However preoccupied we have become with the prospect of winning some opportunity to benefit from free makeovers, most improvement in our lives is the result of hard work on our parts that is not without cost.

It would be easy and exciting if someone else would do the work. But in the end, self-improvement is your job and mine.

## Travel Plans

Dennis the Menace and his parents are apparently headed out of town.

Mom asks Dad, "Are you gonna figure out WHERE WE'RE GOIN', before we get there?"

As Dennis will certainly learn in time, often in life we have to get there before we know where we're going. The inevitable course of events often shapes our ends.

If we want some influence over our destinies, it is always wise to develop a plan for life. Otherwise, we won't know where we're going until we get there. Once we arrive we may well discover it's not at all where we ever wanted to go. We may not have complete control over life, but with a plan, we certainly have more than we would otherwise.

# Otherwise, We Harden

Goethe, the author of *Faust,* once wrote, "We must always change, renew, rejuvenate ourselves; otherwise we harden."

He, of course, is right. Without growth and development, a process of stagnation and decay sets in, robbing life of its vitality and potential. Often, we resist change. But change is a basic element of life. Without it we would all still be infants in our mothers' arms.

Rather than resist, for our own good, we should, as Goethe suggests, continually seek to renew and rejuvenate ourselves; for otherwise, we do harden and die inside before our times.

# Agents of Change

The Indian reformer Mahatma Gandhi once said, "You must be the change you wish to see in the world."

Much in life, without question, could be improved. Every day we all see what change would make better, whether in personal or public life. It is, in fact, easy to find fault and wish things were different. Much harder it is to effect change.

Largely, we expect others to make the difference as though change were not up to us. Gandhi is right. If we want to be better ourselves, if we want conditions to improve, we must be the change we wish to see.

# Blind Hate

We often speak of "blind love," the kind of love that is so enamored with another that it overlooks any fault. But love, really, is never blind. True love sees the faults and failures in others but is strong enough to persevere and overcome, persuaded that another's weaknesses are outweighed by his or her strengths.

In the end, only hate is blind. In order to hate someone, it is necessary to close our eyes to the good in another and see only what we believe is wrong. Only hate fails to see a whole person. And a whole person always possesses some good, even the very worst of us.

The person who straightforwardly hates has failed to see another. For this reason, hate is always a distortion of others. And that is what makes hate, and hate only, blind.

# Cowboy Up

A community activist says that one of her favorite mottos is "Cowboy Up." She goes on to say that for her the expression means ". . . dig deep and find that place within yourself to do what you've set out to do without complaints."

A cowboy's life, even today, can't be easy. Cattle are stubborn. Weather is unpredictable, often hostile, in fact. Markets fluctuate. And there are the perils of disease. Enough to drive anyone to despair.

To fill what seems an almost impossible role, a cowboy must find those hidden reserves of strength to do what must be done, wasting no energy in idle complaint. The cowboy's plight is like life itself. "Cowboy Up" might serve us all with inspiration to persevere.

# The Highway of Life

The comic strip characters Frank and Ernest drive down the highway of life only to hit bump after bump after bump.

Actually, their experience is not unlike our own. On the highway of life, we all hit bumps from time to time. Now and then, it seems that we hit a series of bumps in rapid succession, one right after another.

If the highway of life inevitably presents potholes and protrusions, what might be most important to safe navigation is that we improve our skills of regaining control and avoiding the ditch before we hit the road. Perhaps, we can't avoid bumps; but with preparation, we can avoid disaster.

# Armchair Theologians

I found an advertisement for a series of books for the "armchair theologian." The ad claims the series is "written by experts, but designed for the non-expert."

We all are armchair theologians, no matter what stance toward religion we take, simply because we all wrestle with questions about the meaning and value of life: Why is there something rather than nothing? Why are we here? What does it mean to be a good person and to live a good life? What becomes of us when we die? Whether an atheist or an agnostic or an adherent of some Western religion or Eastern philosophy, we all craft answers to these questions. It simply is in our nature as beings conscious of their existence to raise and answer such "theological" questions. We can't avoid it.

If we all are armchair theologians, we actually could use the help of the experts, those who have thought seriously and systematically about these great questions. Why do we think we don't need them?

# The Things We Treasure Over Time

Mixed throughout the gigantic piles of debris created by major storms are photographs, stuffed animals, rare coins, souvenirs, family heirlooms. Of all that is left behind, these mementos are what people most appreciate.

Nothing actually of great monetary value. But all symbols of the fabric of life so violently torn apart.

Loss does have a way of pointing out to us the things we treasure over time. If only somehow before the crisis, we could live every day in gratitude for and appreciation of life's true treasures.

# Accomplishing Nothing

According to a famous Greek myth, Sisyphus was condemned by the gods to rolling endlessly a stone to the top of a mountain. Each time he reached the summit, the stone rolled back under the force of gravity. And Sisyphus's struggle began again. The ancient Greeks believed that there is no greater punishment than futile labor.

Surveys often indicate how many people are unhappy in their work. Not only is there the drudgery of their labor, but, worse, a sense that they are accomplishing nothing, at least, nothing worthwhile.

Work is often like this. But as one interpreter of the myth of Sisyphus argues, even under the strain of the most laborious work, we human beings have the power to overcome. We need not be defeated in spirit as long as we remember that we choose the spirit in which we do our work. Work may break our backs, but it need not break our spirits. By refusing to be broken by what we do, we actually can find happiness. Certainly, we can triumph.

# Introductory Prayer

According to Sydney Hopkins, writing under the pseudonym Fynn, a young child once began her prayer, saying:

"Mister God, this is Anna."

How many of us, were we to pray, would first have to introduce ourselves? Only occasionally, and often, for some us rarely, do we make any effort to relate ourselves to whatever is divine and transcendent.

And yet, either in the face of some unexpected blessing or in the face of some unanticipated trouble, we cry out in gratitude or despair to those great powers beyond us only for our words to fall back seemingly in silence with no response.

As in any relationship, regular effort to communicate is essential to a sense of contact and intimacy. That constant effort makes introduction unnecessary.

# A Four-Step Plan

I once found an article in a financial planning magazine entitled "A 4-Step Plan to Tackle Credit Card Debt." The four steps:

1. Don't rush into any impulsive arrangements.
2. Examine your situation.
3. List your options, including the pros and cons of each.
4. Pay at least the minimum amount due on all your credit cards.

Upon reflection, it occurred to me that here is a sound plan for life itself. Might we not find life more successful and satisfying if we all were somewhat less impulsive, if we thought about and evaluated our situations, if we weighed our options, and if we acknowledged that nothing worthwhile is achieved without paying our proper dues?

Who, of course, can be sure if this four-step plan would improve our lives? But, as with any problem we tackle, we simply must try to see.

# Back Home

T. S. Eliot in "Little Gidding" has these haunting lines:

We shall not cease from exploration
And the end of all our exploring
Will be to arrive where we started
And know the place for the first time.

It is rather ironic that the place we should know best, and often think we do, is the place we know least and often discover only by leaving. We have a way of taking the familiar for granted. Only when we escape, and unfortunately sometimes only when home is lost, do we really know and appreciate it.

Summer is a season for exploration. But if Eliot is right, it is a time, not just for travel and enjoyment of the exotic, but also a chance to know home and, if by means of comparison only, to appreciate it for the first time.

# Something Like a Star

In one of his most famous poems, Robert Frost offers this prescription:

> So when at times the mob is swayed
> To carry praise or blame too far,
> We may choose something like a star
> To stay our minds on and be staid.

It is quite easy to live life bending to popular opinion. All of us had rather garner praise instead of blame. But popular opinion is fickle and even more often wrong.

For that reason, each of us, if we are to live life well, must set our sights on some standard or principle to guide us, "something like a star" to keep us constant and true and unswayed by the praise and blame of others.

# Good

*Good* is a word we use rather casually today. Most of the time we use it in reference to what feels good.

But when the ancient Greeks used the word, they had in mind what is ultimately good. What is our highest good as human beings? In reply, they almost always proposed some transcendent purpose. In his *Nicomachean Ethics,* Aristotle pondered the good life and the qualities of those who lead it. For the ancient Greeks, good was defined in moral terms.

Clearly, to feel good is not the same as to be good. But true fulfillment may be found only in the latter.

# Manners

In *Life's Little Instruction Book,* a collection of suggestions, observations, and reminders on how to live a rewarding life, this entry appears: "Have impeccable manners."

Today, manners are not much in vogue. Along with chivalry they are dead. But common courtesies like *please* and *thank you* and *excuse me* still have a way of smoothing things and easing relations. They are essential to civilized life.

We may think of them as pretentious, but manners are a way of treating others with respect and kindness. How can life be truly rewarding without them?

# Questions

A respected teacher once said to me, "Always question the answers." He believed, like great minds throughout the ages, that only by questioning the common wisdom of the times and the claims of others do we ever come to the truth.

But we men and women ask questions for different reasons. Occasionally, we ask questions to understand what is immediately unclear and troubling. These questions are asked in respect, not as assertions of personal authority, but in search of the truth. Other times, we ask questions to challenge another's view, not with the motive and intent of learning, but of discrediting another's authority. These questions are born of prejudice and resistance.

In the end, the questions we ask leave us with one overarching question of their own: just how teachable are we? The questions we ask provide the answer.

# Tangles

According to an old maxim, "Never cut what can be untied."

It seems we are always getting ourselves into tangles: disagreements; uncomfortable situations; even conflict, with family, with friends, with co-workers, with neighbors. We often do not know just how to resolve the differences or disagreements and escape the tangled webs our relationships with others so easily become.

Quite often, we resort to some strategy that only makes matters worse. We cut out the tangles of our lives rather than untie them, in part, because that seems easier. It takes time and effort to untie a tangle. But if we untie the tangle rather than cut it out, there is the possibility of starting all over again.

# Night and Day

Included in *Thank You, God! A Jewish Child's Book of Prayers* is this nighttime selection:

Thank you, God, for the day and its work
and the night and its rest.

"Day and its work and the night and its rest" may seem very little for which to be thankful. Too often, we take for granted that we have work to do and that we can sleep at night. Many, of course, have no work to do and spend their days in idleness. And there are those who cannot find rest.

As simple as these gifts are, nonetheless, they are precious blessings and fit subjects of our deepest gratitude.

# Be Somebody

An old poem, written by Virginia Sager, reminds us all in this age that glorifies the body that there is more to us than physical appearance. She writes:

> Be somebody—not just anybody—
> But a body who has grit and grace;
> . . . a body who fills well his place.
>
> Be somebody—not just anybody—
> But a body who always can smile;
> . . . a body who makes life worth while.
>
> Be somebody—not just anybody—
> But a body who'll stand every test;
> . . . a body who gives of his best.

If Sager is right, the old adage "Beauty is only skin deep" may well be just the way it is.

# Point of No Return

*Point of no return.* This commonly used phrase refers to the point in an aircraft's flight at which it no longer has enough fuel to return to its point of departure and must continue on. Used figuratively, it refers to that point at which there is no going back.

Often in life, whether in some new project or in some disagreement with others, we barrel ahead, making no calculation of what will be required if we have to go back. And we find ourselves at a point of no return. There is no going back.

In any enterprise there is true wisdom in estimating where this point may come and determining not to go beyond it so as to court disaster.

# Grief

In a poem on grief entitled "And Thou Art Dead, as Young and Fair," Lord Byron reminds us that there is something in our relationships with those we love that cannot die. It returns to us again and again, and as long as it does, the love we have known only grows.

Byron does not exactly indicate what this something is. But he is sure "dark and dread Eternity" cannot destroy it. I think he has memory in mind.

As long as we remember, those who have departed are not really lost to us. And in remembering, our love for them keeps alive, even grows. The old hymn is right to speak of "precious memories." Their lingering is our tribute to those we have loved.

# Living Deliberately

Remember those now famous words of Thoreau from *Walden; or, Life in the Woods:*

I went to the woods because I wished to live deliberately, to front only the essential facts of life, . . .

Thoreau was determined that he would not come to die only to discover that he had not lived.

Lost it seems in our time is this deliberateness about life. Either we accept the prevalent notions of life's meaning presented in our culture, never testing their truthfulness, or we resign ourselves to life's apparent meaninglessness.

In either case we fail to test life ourselves and to accept the challenge of discovering what there is to life and what we can make of ourselves. If life is to have depth, we have to live, just as Thoreau knew, deeply.

# A Question of Priorities

In "The Arsenal at Springfield," the poet Longfellow suggests:

> Were half the power, that fills the world with
>     terror,
> Were half the wealth, bestowed on camps and
>     courts,
> Given to redeem the human mind from error,
>     There were no need of arsenals or forts:
>
> The warrior's name would be a name abhorred!

In an age of terror, in which security does not seem significantly advanced by the means of warfare, Longfellow's proposition clearly gives us pause. Is it possible that we pursue the end of peace by entirely the wrong means?

Perhaps, results would be more productive and positive if half the power and resources we invest in the means of war were instead invested in the means of peace.

# Assignment

Some terrible tragedy occurs, and our immediate instinct is to ask why. It is in our nature to look for meaning.

In many ways, there is no inherent answer to the question. Suffering, as we recognize at times in our description of it, is meaningless. But it need not remain that way.

It is up to us to give our lives, particularly the terrors and misfortunes that befall us, whatever meaning they may have. We are the meaning-makers. We define life's experiences by our interpretations and responses.

That is our peculiarly human assignment.

# Deal or No Deal?

We often contemplate what role sadness plays in human life. Could life not be, as Charlie Brown once proposed, simply an endless succession of good things, one high followed by another high followed by another high?

We all know that's simply not the way of life, although we don't know quite why life must include trouble as well as fortune.

C. S. Lewis, who married his true love late in life only to lose her after a few years of bliss, puzzled over the question. He determined that there is no rational answer to the question of human suffering. He concluded that pain is part of the pleasure of life, sorrow part of the happiness. That's the deal.

We either accept the deal and make the best of it, or we refuse, merely to compound our misery.

# A Time Beyond Today

Often, trouble hits us with such force that we think it will never end. We fail to remember that we have met with hardship before and have managed to endure. Bad times as well as good times do come and go.

We may not have control over the coming and going of time, but the idea that time passes may be of comfort and encouragement.

Longfellow has the line:

But in ourselves, are triumph and defeat.

Surely, one of our greatest strengths in the face of trouble is the awareness that there is a time beyond today.

# The Company You Keep

I received a greeting card that read:

There is greatness
all around you—
welcome it! It is easy to
be great when you get around you great people.

The card reminded me just how true it is that we are
shaped by the people who surround us. If we surround
ourselves with negative influences, we become negative
ourselves; but, if we choose to associate with positive and
hopeful people, we become like them.

Just as we were taught, we are known by the company
we keep. If we wish to be great people, we must surround
ourselves with greatness.

# Big Problems, Big Opportunities

Not long ago, I discovered this bit of wisdom: "Watch for big problems. They disguise big opportunities."

It's true. What at first seems overwhelming and potentially unconquerable often presents the chance to accomplish something before thought impossible. In many ways, whether it does has to do with how we view matters.

As Francis Bacon once wrote, "A man must make his opportunity, as oft as find it." And finding it means looking for it, sometimes in the most unlikely places.

It is a challenge, but a great sense of fulfillment may lie in rising above some problem and exploiting it for the opportunity it offers. Big problems sometimes are big opportunities.

# Sigh for a Song

To sigh, which may be an ability unique to humans, is to express sorrow, weariness, yearning, or relief merely by a release of breath and to do so often unaware. Indeed, how much we tell with a sigh, far more than words seem to express, unutterable things.

An old hymn bears lyrics that capture our deep desire to exchange a sigh for a song, to replace distress of any kind with an utterance of another kind in a voice joyful and free.

Life, of course, is made of both sighs and songs, each having its proper place. But who does not long to make a trade between the two.

# Clear Beliefs and Firm Principles

Today, in many religious and political circles, the notion that clear beliefs and firm principles will produce positive social change seems widespread. But there may well be something more than mere conviction needed.

And that is what the ancient Greeks called *prudence*—an ability to apply beliefs and principles to actual, real-life situations. Beliefs and principles alone, however clear and firm, are not capable of beneficial results. It is their application to the challenges people face day-to-day that makes the difference.

And that means that our beliefs and principles must be applied with understanding and compassion if they are to produce the results we say we want.

# Hurrying Through Hell

Well you know those times when you feel like
There's a sign there on your back
Says I don't mind if you kick me,
seems like everybody has
Things go from bad to worse
You think they can't get worse than that
And then they do?

Country music artist Rodney Atkins speaks for us all. None of us escapes times when life seems to turn against us, and we are, as Shakespeare puts it, drug "Down, down to hell; . . ."

In such times are we really helpless? Is there nothing we can do? Often, our tendency is to wallow in our troubles. Rather than picking up the pace, we slow down, ruminate over our afflictions, and in so doing become our own tormentors.

Atkins's suggestion is that we do the opposite:

If you're goin' through hell
Walk right through it
You might get out
'Fore the devil even knows you're there.

When we are drug down into some hell, we should get up, get going, and hurry on through.

# Goodbye, Pluto

A group of international astronomers voted no longer to consider Pluto a planet. What Pluto is now is rather vague. Those astronomers who favored Pluto's demotion say that Pluto is a *dwarf planet.*

To mangle Shakespeare, I ask:

> What's in a name? that which we call a planet
> By any other name would be a planet.

My point is that in renaming Pluto nothing about Pluto itself has changed; what has changed is our perception and understanding. We must admit that both perception and understanding, even in the age of scientific objectivity and certainty, are always relative and subject to re-evaluation if we are ever to come to the truth.

# Winding Up the Clock

In Laurence Sterne's humorous novel *The Life and Opinions of Tristam Shandy, Gentleman,* a mother inquires of her son, ". . . have you not forgot to wind up the clock?"

Over time, the steady rhythm of life has a way of depleting both energy and enthusiasm. Its constant pace leaves us often in the need for rejuvenation.

One of the benefits of summer is the opportunity to rewind. A slower pace, a variety in schedule, a break from routine—all allow us the chance to renew. Since summer can be hectic, we must seize the moment to again wind up the clock. Indeed, we must not forget.

# Major

In the course of his or her studies, every college student is expected to declare an academic major, that field in which he or she will concentrate. Quite often, but not always, a major is related to the student's career interests.

All of us have to make similar choices every day. On what will we focus and to what will we give ourselves? We concentrate on the unimportant, and we wonder why our lives seem unfocused and unsuccessful.

The old adage "Don't major in minor things" is actually good advice. If we want to make the most of our lives, we will have to make choices. One key to success is to make those choices in favor of what really is important.

# Creating the Past

In *Heartsongs* Mattie Stepanek, the young victim of a rare form of muscular dystrophy, writes about "Future Reminiscing":

> It is good
> To have a past
> That is pleasant
> To reflect upon.
> Take care
> To create
> Such a gift
> For your future.

If we are to have pleasant pasts to reflect upon, we must do some future planning. After all, we make our pasts today by what we say and do. And to assure that the present will contribute to a pleasant past, we have to plan ahead.

# The Gratitude Attitude

**at·ti·tude** (at′ i tōōd′, -tyōōd′-), *n.* **1.** manner, disposition, feeling, position, etc., with regard to a person or thing; tendency or orientation, esp. of the mind: *a negative attitude; group attitudes.* **2.** position or posture of the body appropriate to or expressive of an action, emotion, etc.: *a threatening attitude; a relaxed attitude.*

As Webster's definition suggests, an attitude is, not just a matter of feeling or thinking, as we commonly assume, but also a way of acting. Nowhere is this more true than in the case of gratitude. A feeling of warm appreciation or a thought of thankfulness is never really complete until it is translated into some appropriate action.

This means that true gratitude requires, not only thought and feeling, but also action. If we don't act out our gratitude, it is incomplete, and we are not as grateful as we think.

# The Music of Life

There is a line in the well-known song "Hey Jude," recorded by the Beatles, which reminds us of an important fact of life. They sing:

Hey Jude, don't make it bad.
Take a sad song and make it better.

Here, the Beatles remind us that much of the time we don't choose the music of life. The style and rhythm of the songs to which our lives are lived are preselected for us, by nature and circumstance. And the very distribution of sad and happy tunes is seldom fair by our standards.

Yet, as "Hey Jude" reminds us, what matters is what we do with the songs assigned to us and whether we make them better.

# Progress

In *A Death in the Desert,* the poet Robert Browning maintains that what is unique about us is our ability to progress. He writes:

> . . . progress, man's distinctive mark alone,
> Not God's, and not the beasts': God is, they are,
> Man partly is and wholly hopes to be.

How true. Most of us would agree that we are only partly what we hope to be. We find ourselves somewhere between promise and reality.

Although Browning's diagnosis could lead to despair about ourselves, it is meant to give us hope. We are creatures who can change. That is why we must persist if we want to make progress.

# Laughter and Tears

Of all creatures, human beings are the only ones who are able to laugh and cry. As someone notes, that is because we are the only creatures who know the difference between what is and what should be.

It is awareness of the incongruity of life that prompts a response of humor or lament. We laugh at what doesn't quite add up. We cry over the failure of life to meet our ideals.

But whether we laugh or cry, humor or tears ought to be the prelude to action intent on lessening life's inconsistencies and disparities, and so, the inspiration to effort on our parts to close the gap between what is and what should be.

# You've Got to Be Taught

One of the songs in the musical *South Pacific* tells of a U.S. Marine lieutenant and a young Tonkinese woman who fall in love, but whose relationship is not accepted by others. The song is entitled "You've Got to Be Carefully Taught." The lyrics run:

> You've got to be taught to be afraid
> Of people whose eyes are oddly made,
> And people whose skin is a different shade,
> You've got to be carefully taught.
> You've got to be taught before it's too late,
> Before you are six or seven or eight,
> To hate all the people your relatives hate,
> You've got to be carefully taught!

It is a song about the sources of hate.

Hate may have many sources. No force as pervasive and powerful as hate can be explained by any single theory. But its continuance generation after generation suggests that whatever hate's sources, we have found successful strategies to bequeath it. Hate is both a defense and an interest we encourage in much of what we say and do. It may be caught, but just as the lyrics of the ballad suggests, it is also taught.

# Aging

Ours is a culture that values youthfulness. Notice advertisements for almost any product on the market and see that they feature vital, attractive youth. But despite all the effort to slow aging, we still grow older. Obviously, it is nature's way.

Why this preference for youthfulness? There are probably many answers. But what is most important is how we think about aging. Is it a forced march into the darkness? Or a pilgrimage into the light?

If we think of this natural process as the way we grow wise and by which we leave behind something that improves the world, it will not seem so frightening to grow old. It will seem to be the way we mature as great souls.

# Avoiding Eyestrain

According to an anonymous quotation, 'There is no danger in developing eyestrain from looking on the bright side of things."

For some reason, most of us are far better at seeing the dark and negative than we are at seeing the bright and positive, whether in people or circumstances. We marvel that life seems to us so unhappy and unsatisfying.

It is all about what we look for. Want to ease the stress and strain of life? Look on the bright side of things. It may surprise you how often you actually see help and hope.

# A Little Better

Reportedly, Franz Kafka commented that the world was one of God's thoughts on one of God's bad days.

The world with all its conflict and inhumanity often looks to observing eyes as an experiment gone tragically wrong. Whatever God's original idea, the world now is far from any divine intention at work in its creation. Any other assessment would be naïve.

But this is not cause for despair. Our challenge is to redeem the world by our own thoughtfulness. Whether the world in the beginning was a bad idea, we can make it better, if only a little. Perhaps, that was God's idea all along.

# Immediately

911. Three simple numbers. Taken separately, numbers of no real significance. Together, they convey a different message. Symbols of some emergency. A matter of urgency, requiring immediate action.

These three numbers are emblematic of what little sense of urgency is left in modern life. Almost nothing arouses in us any sense of immediacy. Life, of course, is full of hurry and haste. Only when life or property seems in jeopardy, do we seem to think any longer that good and right things need to be done without delay—*immediately*.

But whenever we are presented with some opportunity to accomplish the good and do the right thing, quick action is incumbent upon us. As Shakespeare's Macbeth puts it:

If it were done when 'tis done, then 'twere well
It were done quickly: . . .

We best act immediately.

# For Goodness' Sake

A statement attributed to Muhammad, the Islamic prophet, advises:

Acquire knowledge. It enables the possessor to distinguish right from wrong; . . .

The phrase is a clear reminder that the purpose of knowledge is, not only to enrich the mind, but also to inform the heart. We are inclined to think that we learn in order to transform life, making it more convenient and prosperous. And that is true.

But we also study to be transformed ourselves by what we learn. One of the objectives of classical education always has been to shape character, enabling us to distinguish right from wrong. Today's world, perhaps more than ever, requires those who do.

# Continually

It's a children's poem entitled "Peckin'." It reads:

The saddest thing I ever did see
Was a woodpecker peckin' at a plastic tree.
He looks at me, and "Friend," says he,
"Things ain't as sweet as they used to be."

There come moments in life when, to quote the sad subject of these wistful lines, "Things ain't as sweet as they used to be." The marrow seems to have dried up, and life yields her sweet delights sparsely and grudgingly. No amount of effort seems to avail much. And the very reserves from which we commonly draw strength to continue seem depleted. How do we go on?

Our inclinations almost always are to stop. But, maybe, the best course to take is to continue slowly, gradually to peck away. Little in life is accomplished without continual, persistent effort. Diligent performance of duty is usually the key to success.

# The Stuff of Life

Benjamin Franklin, apparently, once posed the question to himself, "Do you love life?" He answered by saying, ". . . do not squander time; for that is the stuff life is made of."

His reply does not seem to answer the question directly. Maybe, indirectly it does. How could anyone who truly loves life squander time. Time may be spent fruitfully in any number of ways, working or playing or resting. But it should never be squandered, wasted to no meaningful end.

Franklin, who spent time in a variety of ways and was as productive as anyone, could work and play and rest. But he seemed to understand that to squander the stuff of life is the ultimate expression of disdain for life itself.

# Fall

There's a kind of hush that comes over the landscape in late October. A quiet and calm like that at the end of day when work is done.

It is most apparent early morning and late evening. It is a quiet and calm that leaves the alert person with an unusual peace. It is the peculiar spirit of fall.

Fall days are a time to soak in that spirit of quiet and calm and to be renewed by the constant cycle of the seasons and the blessings nature itself brings.

# Habit

It is a word we no longer favor. Today, we talk of *motive*—that immediate impulse to say or do what we think some circumstance requires. When we do think of the word, it usually is in reference to what we think of as persistent bad behavior.

But the word *habit* is still useful, even more so today than ever. According to Aristotle, a habit is some settled disposition to say or do what's good. A habit is the result of sufficient practice, so that when some word or deed is required, it occurs almost automatically.

Motives can change with time. Habits prevail. That is exactly why it is so important to practice good behavior from the start and make it a matter of habit.

# Task or Title

Perhaps, it always has been, but prestige is an important value in modern culture. Renown based on achievement drives much of human striving today. Best schools, best jobs, best neighborhoods—all seem to be what people now want.

But tasks still remain more important than titles. Titles may enhance self-esteem, but tasks, especially when well-done, are what make for a better world.

And that's what is most important. Not our reputations, but our contributions.

# The Last Thing I Do

"Die, my dear Doctor, that's the last thing I shall do." So Lord Palmerston reportedly proclaimed on his deathbed. Clever and true. Death is the last act in every human drama.

The ancient Greeks held to the idea that the true nature of a thing is not known until the end. In dying we may reveal more about ourselves than we ever do in life.

But since none of us knows the day or the hour of this last act, the best strategy is to live each moment well, concentrating on important things. That may be the only guarantee that we will die well.

# Catch-Up

It had been a long and difficult climb up the perilous peak. The Sherpas had led their Western climbers for several grueling days. Suddenly, midafternoon on the fourth day, they simply stopped and sat down.

The climbers asked, "Why?" The Sherpas answered that the travel had been, not only hard, but fast. They explained, "We must now let our souls catch up with our bodies."

In life the pace, often, is so quick that keeping up in mind is more difficult than keeping pace in body. Now and again, as the Sherpas understood in this popular story, we need respite and time for our souls to catch up.

It is time we must take for our own well-being.

# Burying the Past

It's a sage recommendation:

In the very depths of yourself, dig a grave. Let it be like some forgotten spot to which no path leads; and there, in the eternal silence, bury the wrongs that you have suffered. Your heart will feel as if a weight had fallen from it, and a divine peace comes to abide with you.

Too often, we carry with us the painful and disabling memories of past wrongs done us, which nothing we can now do will erase. Our memories of them serve no purpose but to unsuit us for the present.

If we have made whatever remedy we can, and if we have learned what we can from our hurts, the only remaining good we can do is to let them go—especially, if we want to find peace.

# Understanding

A major communications company once adopted as its slogan "To communicate is the beginning of understanding."

Today, if anything is needed in the world, it is understanding—between people and among nations. The first step is to communicate.

But communication is not just talking; it is also listening. True understanding comes only when, in addition to expressing our views, we listen intently to the views of others, especially the views of those with whom we differ. It has been said so often that it now seems trite, but communication is a two-way street. Traffic must pass in both directions for there to be understanding.

# Just Coincidence

Some time ago, I received one of those memorable, somewhat laughable, greeting cards. From the cover a scruffy canine speaks:

"There must be some kind of mystical telepathic link between us. Just the other day I was in a store reading a card, and I thought of you . . . ."

Inside the monologue continues:

". . . and now you are reading the same card and thinking about me! (It's got to be more than just coincidence!)"

Well, of course. No matter how much we wish it were true, seldom do others know we are thinking of them by mere telepathy. Goodness is not a simple matter of right thought; right action is required to make goodness real.

Thinking of someone? Better do something to let the person know.

# Becoming a Name

Naming newborns has become something of an industry in recent times. Prospective parents have access to authors who research the popularity of names and publish their results to guide parents in their choices. There are even professional nameologists now who can be employed for several hundred dollars to help with the selection.

In some primitive cultures, the custom is to wait and to name a child after it is clear what the child's nature is and to select a name that reflects that nature. A child may not be named for several years until just the right name is clear.

All of us, actually, make our own names, at least what our names stand for. The poet Tennyson in "Ulysses" has the line:

. . . I am become a name; . . .

The currency of names is passing; what matters is what we make of our names through time and what values those names come to represent.

# How We Live

In James Boswell's *The Life of Samuel Johnson,* Dr. Johnson has the line, "It matters not how a man dies, but how he lives."

We are easily struck these days by the pageantry of the funerals of the rich and famous. They lend an ambiance to the lives of those remembered, which may or may not be deserved on the grounds of how they actually lived. Often, we fail to understand that the only true eulogy is the life someone lives, and at death, nothing can be added to or taken from it. It is a testament written everyday.

And so, Dr. Johnson is right:

It matters not how a man dies, but how he lives. The act of dying is not of importance, it lasts so short a time.

# Like the Dew

The dew falls softly and quietly at night when all nature rests. Although it is a relatively small quantity of moisture, it is just enough to refresh the earth.

We, who are often restless and impatient, might find in finer things, not the coarser things of life we so often pursue, our own refreshment. What works quietly can work mightily. But then we, like nature itself, must be quiet and patient, allowing the still dew to relieve our troubled minds and hearts.

The prophet Hosea writes of the Divine, "I will be as the dew . . . ." Oh, if we would only be still long enough to know such priceless blessing.

# Better, Not Bigger

We've come to think bigger is better. It is as though we simply assume that size or number is the preeminent measure of quality. Bigger houses, bigger cities, bigger meals—all must be better. Want to improve something, simply super-size it.

But bigger is not better. Only better is better. Quantity is not quality. If we want better things, we must work to make them better, not simply bigger.

And so, if there is a way to the better, it may well not be the way of the bigger. At least, we shouldn't assume it is.

# Keeping Rhythm

Rhythm is the regular recurrence of some element, from the pattern of pulses in music, to the repetition of the seasons, to the beat of the human heart.

One of our rare human traits is the ability to keep rhythm, both as individuals and groups, by synchronizing our own actions with established patterns. Much of the time we seem out of rhythm with the forces of life, and the result is a detrimental disharmony.

But we do know, even if the experience is rare, the delight and peace of keeping rhythm, by aligning ourselves with nature and with others. In such moments, perhaps, we are in sync with the very rhythms of the universe, and we fulfill our destinies.

# Weird

The Welsh social reformer Robert Owen somewhere said, "All the world is [weird] save [you] and me, and even [you] are a little [weird]." Owen reportedly said these words to a business partner with whom he severed ties.

The words themselves represent a tendency we all have. It is to judge others by our own preferences, as though we had no idiosyncrasies ourselves. On occasion we do so good-naturedly, but other times we do so with little toleration and to the final detriment of relationships, just as Owen did with his partner.

Since we all have our peculiarities, maybe, we should not judge so harshly what strikes us as weird. No doubt, to somebody somewhere, something about us seems just as weird.

# Hands

Composed of twenty-seven bones, tissue, and sinew, available in two complimentary versions, right and left, they are, perhaps, among the most complicated and functional tools ever fashioned: hands.

We can hold hands, fold hands, sit upon our hands, or open our hands. These are our choices. Much of the quality of our own lives and the very condition of the world depend upon what we decide.

The Quakers seem to have understood the importance of what we do with our hands. "Hands to work, hearts to God," they said. It is still true: the best way to serve what is holy and divine is to put our hands to work in noble enterprise.

# Some Words of Advice

One author calls them "an ascending order of ethical commitment." This order encapsulates the moral teachings of some of the world's most famous figures:

Socrates: "Know thyself."
Aristotle: "Control thyself."
Jesus: "Give thyself."

If the moral advice of the ages could be summarized in three phrases, perhaps these are the three. People of good character know themselves. They have an understanding of their strengths and weaknesses. This familiarity with themselves enables them to control themselves and restrain their tendencies to act from weakness. And knowing and controlling themselves, they are able to make of themselves something worth sharing with others.

These simple phrases may well constitute, not only "an ascending order of ethical commitment," but an ascending scale of human excellence. And ascending that scale may well be what life is really all about.

# Useless Grumbling

The Wisdom of Solomon warns, "Beware then of useless grumbling, . . ."

Language may well serve other, certainly higher, uses, but we humans frequently rely upon its power simply to grumble about life in general and in particular.

Grumbling may serve to discharge some measure of our discontent, but seldom does it produce constructive results. Worse, grumbling often proves a trap: the more we grumble, the more we grumble. What energy we might have to amend our lives and circumstances is consumed nonproductively in a downward spiral of complaint.

It was for this reason, perhaps, the author of the Wisdom of Solomon linked the words "useless" and "grumbling." There may be some form of useful complaining, but surely it is rare. If we wish to have better lives and improved circumstances, our energy must be invested, not in "useless grumbling," which changes nothing and worsens much, but in constructive action.

# In Memoriam

Memories are precious. Because we can remember, our lives have continuity through time, and we are not always obliged to learn life's lessons again and again.

Memories are also the means by which we keep what is important in our lives even after the important is gone. Someone has argued that often a friend or family member is really closer to us in memory than he or she was in life. In life we were apt to take that person's presence for granted, allowing many a day to go by without so much as a thought of the other.

But at times after another's death, we think daily of the person we have loved. Consequently, through memory that person is constantly with us, kept close by recollection.

That is the blessing of memory: as long as we remember, someone gone is not really lost to us, but lives on.

# Today

The words are attributed to Martial, written sometime in the first century CE:

> . . . wise men don't say
> 'I shall live to do that',
> tomorrow's life is too late;
> live today.

Most of the time, we are either looking back or looking ahead, preoccupied with regret or fear. Even when we are glad and grateful, it is because of something that has happened or we expect to happen.

But, although we are blessed as human beings with memory and hope, the only moment we really have is now. And the only moment we can affect for better or worse is the present one. That is why the wise live today.

# Good Company

Supposedly, so I have read, when he lived in New York as a child, Theodore Roosevelt was advised to select carefully those boys with whom he played. He was told in effect:

Remember this always: there are only two classes of boys, good boys and bad boys. If you choose your companions among the good boys, you need not worry whether they are rich or poor, or who their fathers and mothers are.

Here is wise counsel for all who want to surround themselves with good company. Far more important than status or ancestry in choosing friends is character. It doesn't matter what side of town someone comes from, rather what side he or she takes on moral issues.

Choose friends with this criterion in mind, and you will always find yourself in good company.

# Crowded Out

In the busy and hectic pace of life, so often what is really important gets crowded out by less significant things. A review of almost any given week reveals how much time was spent working, fulfilling community commitments, completing routine tasks—many of no lasting value.

These are important and, of course, even necessary. But without effort, they can easily take over life. And suddenly family, friends, leisure, self-enrichment lose place. In many ways, we are shaped by what we make time for. And so, to use the words of a tune of a former era, each of us must ask, is "Time . . . on my side"? Does the distribution of time in my life make for a better me or a me less than the best I can be?

Maybe, some crowd control is required. And that job falls to us.

# The Secret to Happiness

According to a study, Americans are not the happiest people in the world; the Danes are. Interestingly, the Danes have lower annual incomes than Americans and generally live less affluent lives.

Surprising. We Americans have assumed and staked our lives on the assumption that happiness depends on having—having more wealth, power, prestige. Apparently, what we Americans value most is not the secret to our happiness.

What the Danes value is having enough—more and more people having enough. They believe collective responsibility, belonging, and leisure make for happiness.

And so, we Americans must ask if we have not put our hopes in the wrong place in our search to be happy.

# Still the Best

Increasingly in modern life, we seem willing to accept mediocrity. The ordinary, the average, the commonplace are acceptable to us. As the word *mediocrity* itself implies, the middle range is simply enough. OK is now quite sufficient. The pursuit of excellence is derided as some sick form of perfectionism.

But all great achievement, whether in art or science, is the result of not settling for the simply OK. A culture that ceases to strive for the best fates itself to decay. All betterment of the human condition depends on pressing beyond the present limits of human accomplishment.

In the poem "The Lie," probably written by Sir Walter Raleigh, there is the line:

Fear not to touch the best; . . .

Indeed, not only fear not, fail not.

# Awake, Sleepers!

In *The Family Circus,* Dolly awakes from sleep to declare to her mother, "Mom, I had the best dream last night. I just hate that I slept through it."

It is, of course, natural to sleep through our nocturnal dreams, but, too often, in our waking hours, we do the same. Diurnal inspirations stir our spirits, but we seldom act on them. We might as well be asleep.

Thoreau once asserted, "I have never yet met a man who was quite awake." Much of the time, we sleep-walk through life, failing to heed the higher callings of our dreams. We, like the poet Langston Hughes, should ask, "What happens to a dream deferred?" Dreams beg active effort to be realized. Implicit in their presence is the command, "Awake, sleepers!" Dreams really are meant to come true.

# Decisions

A health magazine offers some advice on making decisions. Among the author's suggestions are:

Define the problem.
Identify your values.
Plan a course of action.

It is a simple strategy, really.

Often, we seem paralyzed by decision. Naturally, it is not always easy to decide, but nothing is worse than failing to choose a course of action and proceeding. As political activists of the sixties often said, using an aphorism they did not create, but whose truth they understood, "Not to decide is to decide."

Since time waits on no one, it is far better to find some method for making decisions and then go forward.

# Hospitality

Holidays provide a season for practicing the ancient, but almost lost, virtue of hospitality.

In the busy rush of life, there hardly seems time to invite guests into our homes and to go to great lengths to make them feel honored and welcomed. In the past, people very often felt it a special privilege to welcome guests, present to them their best, and treasure them for their very presence.

Perhaps, we might all make the holiday season even more memorable for others by adding to our affairs an exorbitant graciousness, by adding an ungrudging hospitality.

# Heritage

According to a story I've read, a precious vase, made by a skilled artisan, was passed down generation after generation among a New England family. Each custodian charged with its care placed the vase in a prominent position in his or her home. The vase almost became an object of worship.

One afternoon a mother came home to be met at the door by her daughter.

"Momma," she said, "remember that vase passed down from generation to generation in our family?"

"Yes," her mother replied.

"Well," the daughter continued, "this generation just dropped it."

Heritage seems only slightly regarded today. But tradition and custom are what give life continuity. The wisdom of the ages means each generation need not repeat the mistakes of the past. Whenever we are tempted to despise the past and reject the insight of history, we doom ourselves to error and injury entirely avoidable. The calling of each generation is to perpetuate and transfer the best to those who come after.

# The Longest Pleasure

In *Don Juan* Lord Byron writes:

Now hatred is by far the longest pleasure;
Men love in haste, but they detest at leisure.

The lines truly reveal something about human nature. Pleasures of any kind, material or spiritual, seem only temporary and fleeting. All our efforts to make them last, which can be considerable, seem doomed to failure.

But with seemingly no effort, we can harbor and perpetrate hatred in its many forms almost forever. Even our best efforts seldom remove our sense of offence or injury and the disdain we feel in response to the harm others do us.

Could Byron be right? Are the ill-will and contempt we so easily carry, in the end, a source of pleasure for us? A delight in our detest of others?

Maybe. Perhaps, hatred is sadistic in its true nature. And for that reason, we must detest in ourselves whatever pleasure we get in blaming and despising others.

# What's Wrong with the World?

The *Times of London* some years ago requested a number of imminent authors and thinkers to submit essays on the question, what's wrong with the world? The famous journalist and religious writer G. K. Chesterton submitted the shortest and, perhaps, most profound reply. He wrote:

Dear Sirs:

I am.

Sincerely yours,
G. K. Chesterton

Most of us would agree that there is much wrong with the world, but few of us seem to acknowledge our parts. We assume that the world's problems lie at the feet of everyone else, and that we make no contribution to what's wrong with the world.

The world would, if only in small ways, be a better place if we accepted responsibility for our personal shares of the burden of the world's ills and if we set about to make things better in our own corners.

# And Yet

In *All Rivers Run to the Sea: Memoirs,* the famous holocaust writer Elie Wiesel states that, of all the words in the English language, his favorite two are the words *and yet.* He illustrates: "The sun is rising? And yet it will set. A night of anguish? And yet it too, will pass." The words, he says, are a constant reminder to him that everything has its time, and nothing is forever, whether pleasure or pain.

In the course of life, it is certainly true that all things have their rhythm. There is a cycle of birth, maturity, and, eventually, death. Neither life's happiness nor its sadness and pain are immune. Everything we experience is followed by some "and yet," as Elie Wiesel reminds us.

Wiesel concludes that the lesson this natural cycle teaches us is that we should "shun resignation" and "refuse to wallow in fatalism." We should make the most of everything we experience. Enjoy to the fullest the joys of the moment and profit as much as possible from moments of life's troubles. They all pass with time. And so, two words—and yet. They apply to every circumstance of life, happy or bleak. A reminder that everything has its season, and nothing is forever.

# Thanksgiving

It's a November custom. We will gather around tables perfectly set and laden with well-prepared foods of the season. In the company of family and friends, we will dine sumptuously.

In today's world, we haven't the sense we used to have that food does not just appear in the market and on the table. It must be grown. It is the produce of unseen labor and long months of anxiety and hope.

Even less, do we think that some miracle of mercy and goodness is involved throughout the natural cycle of the seasons, from planting to harvesting, and that there is an invisible presence to be credited and thanked for what seems almost automatically to appear before us. Food is a gift and one deserving of true thanksgiving.

# Foundations of Friendships

Despite our intentions and best efforts, every so often friendships, instead of sustaining us, end in silence and bitterness. Perhaps, it is because they are founded upon superficial grounds.

In his obscure play *Timon of Athens,* Shakespeare writes of a wealthy noble who has many friends as long as he is generous toward them. But his friends were interested only in what he could offer them. When his resources were spent, his would-be friends abandoned him, criticizing him for not being more responsible with his money.

According to Aristotle, there are three kinds of friendship: friendship based on mutual usefulness, friendship based on common interests, and friendship based on shared values. It is the last of these that is most satisfying and most likely to endure.

# Roadblocks

None of us likes impediments to progress. Obstacles that delay or divert us along the way in any project are seldom viewed well, but are often despised and resisted.

Roadblocks periodically help, preventing us from plunging headlong into disaster. Instead of assuming we should not be impeded, perhaps, when something slows our paces or diverts our efforts, we would do well to ask if we should not slow down or take another course altogether to advance.

The thirteenth century Archbishop of Canterbury Stephen Langton prayed, "Come, Holy Spirit, . . . guide what goes off the road."

Maybe, at least sometimes, there is guidance at work in what sends us off course.

# The Ultimate Choice

We make many choices in the courses of our lives: what to wear, where to eat, whom to marry, which job to take. The significance of these choices, of course, varies. Some are of little consequence; some are life-changing.

But the most important choice each of us makes is how to live this life. Ironically, it often receives less consideration than any of the other choices we make. What is the good life? is the most essential of all human questions. What we stand up for and are willing to sacrifice to achieve are at stake.

Here is the ultimate choice. The choice really worth thought. If character is destiny, then the fates of our lives depend upon our answers.

# The Immensity of Little Things

In his May 21, 2004, column, "A Dash of Comma Sense," George F. Will wrote about the importance of punctuation to meaning. He cited a number of examples of the very significance the placement of something as small as a comma has on the meaning of a sentence. That's the power of little things.

Today, we are inclined to think that only big things matter, and the bigger the things, the bigger the difference they make. But little things also matter, often, just as much as their larger competitors. A smile, a kind word, a helpful gesture can make the difference in the quality of the day.

Maybe, the time has come to consider the immensity of little things and give them their due.

# Redeployment

In "Ulysses," Alfred, Lord Tennyson writes of the mixed emotions we humans know when some chapter of our lives comes to an end, and we are left, if only temporarily, unemployed:

> How dull it is to pause, to make an end,
> To rust unburnished, not to shine in use,
> As though to breathe were life!

The boredom and uselessness in such times seem to call into question our very sense of purpose.

But Tennyson offers hope:

> . . . but something ere the end,
> Some work of noble note, may yet be done, . . .

Clearly, the challenge we meet in facing what ends is to find that "work of noble note," and so, not to retire, but to redeploy. And if we do, we may yet "shine in use."

# Yesterday

They are lyrics of a still popular song by the Beatles:

Yesterday, all my troubles seemed so far away.
Now it looks as though they're here to stay.
Oh, I believe in yesterday.

No doubt, today may not seem as happy and hopeful as yesterday. But the answer to today's troubles is not, as the lyrics suggest, to dwell on yesterday. The opposite is true. And that is to think about tomorrow.

Not only is tomorrow the only day that can bring what's better, focusing on yesterday is a sure formula for missing any happy prospects. Hold yesterday in memory, but work on tomorrow. Indeed, as the lyrics of Fleetwood Mac's *Don't Stop* suggest:

Don't stop, thinking about tomorrow, . . .

Especially, when today is not as good as yesterday.

# All the Things We Take for Granted

Homes, food, health, family, friends, the very gift of life—all things we take for granted. But, in the end, they are the very things of which life is made. Only a moment's reflection will prove how valuable and essential they are and what life would be without them.

Thanksgiving is a season to remember with glad and grateful hearts all those things that are present all the time and that sustain us from day to day.

All the things we take for granted are really our truest blessings.

# Good, Better, Best

We learned the words in school as degrees of something desirable: *good, better, best.* But good, better, best are more than language used for comparison. Good, better, best are realities of everyday life.

Life confronts us with choices, not just between good and evil, but choices among degrees of goodness. While we should never despise or undervalue anything good, we should recognize that some things are better than others, and always aspire for the best of things.

Indeed, without high standards little good is achievable. As the English poet Robert Browning put it in "Andrea del Sarto,"

Ah, but a man's reach should exceed his grasp, . . .

Often, it is the quest for the best that results in what is good, even what is better.

# Failed Resolutions

We made them with every good intention and determination to keep them. So soon, now, we have failed to fulfill them. Ever question why our "great and mighty resolutions" so often seem to end in other than "great actions"?

Samuel Johnson, one of the greatest figures in literature, apparently also found resolutions more easily made than kept. A 1775 diary entry records the despair he experienced over his inability to reform his life. His failure was most upsetting. He wrote:

> When I look back upon resolutions of improvement and amendments, which have year after year been made and broken, either by negligence, forgetfulness, vicious idleness, casual interruption or morbid infirmity; . . . why do I yet try to resolve again?

He then replies:

> I try because reformation is necessary, and despair is criminal; I try, in humble hope of the help of God.

In effect, although he most often met with failure, he continued to resolve to improve himself and to amend his life; to do otherwise was not to try at all. And that's as good a reason for us to resolve again as well.

# No Reflection on You

How often in the course of rendering some complaint or making some criticism, we have sought to avoid any offense to present company by saying, "No reflection on you"?

We don't mean to direct our criticisms or complaints at present company. Maybe, we simply have spoken before thinking. But one thing is sure. Our criticism and complaints are a reflection upon us.

They reveal our own views and values, which quite often are nothing more than petty preferences and prejudices, and our tendencies to assume we stand at the center of the universe. Of course, we don't. Perhaps, we should think twice about proclaiming what we like and what we don't like before we speak, since what we praise and what we blame does reflect upon us.

# Ain't No Way

According to recording star Toby Keith, there "Ain't no right way, / To do the wrong thing, . . ." As he elaborates:

> You can justify,
> But it's still black and white,
> Paint it any shade,
> But it won't change
> Ain't no right way
> To do the wrong thing.

Whether it is the choice to keep or give a child away, resort to violence in domestic life, permit or deny prayer in public school, from Keith's moral point of view, the answers are clear and compelling. Between the white of right and the black of wrong, there are no shades of gray. We ". . . can justify, / but it's still black and white, . . ."

Perhaps, in some matters this is the case, and from some absolute and universal moral perspective, it is true in all cases. But moral life as we know it and have to live it is far more ambiguous than Keith seems to think. And that's why most of the world's great moral traditions caution us against moral arrogance and self-righteousness. Is there ever a right way to do the wrong thing? I don't know. But this I do know: there is a wrong way to do the right thing, and that may be the gravest moral danger we face.

# Nothing More than Feelings

A cemetery is the place. And the conversation only two sentences.

"He was a really down-to-earth guy," a would-be comforter says to her friend.

"That's a bit more condolence than I need right now," the bereft widow replies.

No matter what we think, it is never possible to guess someone else's feelings. And yet, we expect others to do it all the time. Without so much as providing a clue, we expect people, especially those close to us, to read our thoughts and know our feelings and to say and do the perfectly fitting thing.

As the *Wizard of Id* reminds us in the scenario above, we, and not others, are responsible for our feelings. If we want those around us to know and understand and help us, we will have to help them first. We will simply have to tell them what we think and feel. Otherwise, they will never know.

# Tree of Loveliness and Peace

Millions all over the world will decorate their homes with Christmas trees this holiday season.

No one quite knows the origin of this custom. According to one legend, people in Scandinavia once worshiped trees. When Scandinavians became Christians, they made evergreen trees part of their Christian festivals. It was the Germans who probably first adorned Christmas trees with decorations. They decorated the trees with nuts and candies wrapped in bright papers. Later, they added tinsel. Martin Luther, many believe, was the first to use lights on a tree at Christmas to represent the glory and beauty of the stars above Bethlehem on the night of Christ's birth.

Today, beautifully decorated trees stand in our homes at Christmas, pointing toward heaven, reminding us how God so long ago came down in the form of Bethlehem's babe and in Christ is with us still. Their branches so lovely, reaching out to us, calling us to be faithful, true, and to trust in God in all we do.

# Too Much Talk

Somewhere, the Chinese philosopher Chuang Tzu contends:

A dog is not considered a good dog because he is a good barker. A man is not considered a good man because he is a good talker.

Master Chuang expresses a view held by many of the world's sages, and it is that there is virtue in silence and, often, vice in saying too much.

There always has been a certain charm to worldly talk. We like to talk about ourselves, and we like to hear talk of other people's lives. But unrestrained talk of others and indiscriminate talk of ourselves very often breed only malice and pride.

In a time of almost constant chatter, much of it uncharitable and some of it no more than pure ignorance, there truly may be too much talk.

# Life's Best Prize

Theodore Roosevelt in his 1903 speech at the annual fair of the New York State Agricultural Association said, "Far and away the best prize that life offers is the chance to work hard at work worth doing, . . ."

We don't always think of work as a blessing. It can, in fact, often be mere drudgery, at times even meaningless. Yet, just imagine life without any work to do. Endless hours of leisure would soon become monotonous and boring.

As Roosevelt suggests, life's best prize may well be "the chance to work hard at work worth doing." Decent work, not only enriches the worker's life, but contributes to the greater good of the community. But decent work alone is not enough. In addition, industry is required to make work beneficial to our lives and to others. And industry is not a matter of chance. We decide whether we will work hard at what we do. Even decent work is unrewarding unless we give it our very best efforts.

## To Stare

I was taught as a child that it is impolite to stare. And usually it is.

But there may be an exception to this general rule of good behavior, and this is the very season to acknowledge it. Shakespeare captures the mystery of these days in now famous lines spoken by Marcellus to Horatio:

Some say that ever 'gainst that season comes
Wherein our Saviour's birth is celebrated,
The bird of dawning singeth all night long:
And then, they say, no spirit dares stir abroad;
The nights are wholesome; then no planets strike,
No fairy takes, nor witch hath power to charm,
So hallow'd and so gracious is the time.

There is something magical, mystical about this time of year. A peace and calm descend, and goodness abounds all around. This "so hallow'd and so gracious" time of year, we might all stop and stare—and wonder.

# Signs of the Times

Tinsel and trees, wreaths and glitter, lights and music— they are all signs of the times. The great occasion of Christmas approaches.

Much of the time, we never know what's ahead, but this time of year is the exception. It's merriment and mirth we anticipate. And the signs are our assurance that they are near. The expectation is part of the excitement.

If we intend and work toward what we hope for, the likelihood is that our expectations will indeed come true, and we will again know the special joy and peace of this season.

# The Way Things Turn Out

According to a popular saying, "Things turn out best for those who make the best of the way things turn out." The logic may be suspect, but the truth is unassailable.

So often in life, we stand passively in the face of factors we cannot control. We lament that circumstances are not what they should be, and complain we can do nothing. No doubt, conditions are often unfavorable to our purposes, and many things we cannot change.

But the challenge in life is to make the best of whatever is. Waiting for the ideal is generally a waste of time and opportunity. In the face of what we wish were different, the task at hand is to make the most of what is. That may be the only way things turn out for the best.

# What If?

An ad Starbucks ran before the 2008 election raised the question:

What if we cared all of the time the way we care some of the time? What if we cared when it was inconvenient as much as we care when it is convenient? Would your community be a better place? Would our country be a better place? Would our world be a better place?

Who can answer with anything but a resolute, "Yes!"

If the passion we have and express when unsettled by social, political, or economic issues were translated into constructive effort, which seems seldom if ever to occur, what better places our communities, our country, and the world would be. Life is changed, not so much by mere thought and feeling, but by hard work. And hard work brings its greatest results over time with consistent, persistent effort. What would be the result "if we cared all of the time" and did what needs to be done?

# Peace A-Coming

This is the season of peace, so we say. A claim now and then hard to believe. All around, life seems unsettled.

The fact is any Christmas season is not unlike the first. It was into a violent world, the Christ Child first came—a world of political turmoil and military oppression, a world not unlike our own.

Perhaps, unrest and conflict threaten the spirit of the season. Circumstances, however, only make the message of this special season more important, not less—the great hope of peace a-coming.

# No Crib for a Bed

The ancient story claims he was born in a cattle stall. A rude beginning, no doubt. Yet, a reminder to us all that infants have always come into the world in less than auspicious circumstances.

And a challenge to us to work to end those conditions that fate the young from the start. Infants, whatever their status, deserve warmth and care and the best from the very beginning.

That holy child, whose birth we celebrate this season, is not honored until all children are honored. And that is the task to which we are still called—two thousand years later.

# When Your Name Is Your Title

People often construct their identities and assess their worth as individuals around their titles. A name alone, they seem to think, hardly conveys much prestige. It appears, to be somebody, it is necessary by modern standards to have a name with a prefix: Doctor, President, Pastor, Chairman, Reverend. Indeed, many people are offended if addressed without use of title.

When assigned the task to free the Israelites from slavery in Egypt, Moses inquired of God what he should say if anyone asked him God's name. God replied, "I AM WHO I AM. . . . This is my name forever, and this my title for all generations."

Although an identification of name and title as one is entirely appropriate and expected in the case of God, it may well be appropriate for people, too. When you and I can dispense with the pretension of titles, and it is true of us that our names are our titles, then we have come to know who we are and have found true human worth.

# Forgive Us Our Christmases

The hustle and bustle of Christmas shopping, the addressing and mailing of Christmas cards, the hurried preparations for dinners and parties of the season, and wrapping of packages—all make for rather tired bodies and frayed nerves.

The story of one little girl seems to illustrate the case with us all. The day before Christmas, apparently, as it is in many households, had been a particularly hectic one. Her mother ran nervously all day long, impatient of any interruptions from her daughter. The father was equally harried by a list of little duties and had no time for a child. She was just in everybody's way all day, until she was at last ushered upstairs to bed. All the excitement had taken its toll on her, too. When she knelt by her bed to pray the Lord's Prayer, she was so confused and distraught that she actually prayed, "Forgive us our Christmases as we forgive those who Christmas against us."

I sometimes think that Christmas is something we do to each other and to ourselves, robbing ourselves and others of all the joy and peace it portends, and that we really ought to ask to be forgiven. Again and again, we let the hustle and bustle crowd out the real purpose and meaning of Christmas. Maybe, we should slow down and give Christmas the chance to just happen to us.

# Christmas Peace

According to reports of the Christmas Truce of 1914, British and German troops put down their guns and celebrated peacefully together in no man's land between the trenches. Briefly, the war came to a halt. Festivities began in some places when German troops lit candles on the Christmas trees on their parapets. The British sentries a few hundred yards away could see them. Elsewhere, it was reported that the British acted first by starting bonfires and letting off rockets. "Just you think," wrote one British soldier, "that while you were eating your turkey, etc., I was out talking and shaking hands with the very men I had been trying to kill a few hours before!! It was astounding!"

Can't but ponder, really. If then, why not now? If on Christmas, why not every day? If peace at Christmas, why not all year 'round?

# Dark as Winter

*Winter* is, not only the word by which we identify the coldest season of the year, but the very symbol of all that is dreary and dark in life, of any time of toil or trouble. T. S. Eliot memorialized the phrase "dead of winter" in his poem "Journey of the Magi." Certainly, there are severe winters, tedious and full of discontent in every life.

The severest of winters, from which we all need the relief of spring, is often that of our own hearts. Whether with disappointment or resentment or despair, our hearts become cold and dark, like winter itself.

But hidden in this season, when

> Frosty wind [makes] moan,
> Earth [stands] hard as iron, . . .

is the promise of relief. The very words we say and the songs we sing tell of a time when winter will be past. And that is the great hope.

# Conviction

William Butler Yeats writes:

> Things fall apart; the center cannot hold;
> Mere anarchy is loosed upon the world, . . .
> The best lack all conviction, while the worst
> Are full of passionate intensity.

There are times in our affairs—both in the affairs of individuals and groups—when what we have found faithful in the past seems to have failed and no longer is reliable. Yeats describes these times of our lives as "anarchy."

But Yeats knows, not only the anarchy of such moments, but of the seeming loneliness they impose. Often, when "things fall apart," we are left without the company of our best allies, and all alone we face the fierce attack of our worst and most passionate detractors.

In the worst of times, when we are caught in the crosswinds of conflict, there is a center that holds and steadies us. It is conviction. Not the conviction of others, but our own. Conviction, not merely our cherished beliefs, but our most firmly held values, remains a true companion, and offers, perhaps, even a way to persevere and ultimately overcome.

Conviction requires of us our best in the worst of times, especially when "things fall apart."

# Unfinished Business

The film *A Late Quartet,* featuring Christopher Walken and the late Philip Seymour Hoffman, recounts the struggle of four talented musicians to sustain their ensemble in the face of their leader's battle with Parkinson's disease and the inevitability of his retirement. The impending transition reveals long-standing tensions among the four. They threaten the quartet's very survival.

What, in the end, proves the quartet's salvation is the willing surrender of its members' personal interests for the higher good and the continuation of what matters most, their music. Ambition and enmity, even devotion and familiarity are transcended, and the quartet survives, although in a different form. Throughout most of the film, the prospect of personal transcendence and the quartet's continuation seem unlikely, but finally, both are achieved.

This is life's most important business: to rise above our individual pursuits for the triumph of some higher good. As of yet, this work is unfinished business.

# Postscript

Aristotle, a Greek philosopher of the fourth century BCE, was convinced that the preeminent question every human being faces and all humankind must address is that of what is the good life and what are the qualities of those who lead it. The life of every person and of every community is a narrative reply. We write the lines of the human conversation. And our lives and the collective stories of our communities answer Aristotle's question.

*Lifelines* presents Aristotle's question in some of its various dimensions and offers some responses we can and do make as we write the lines of our own stories and shape the lives of those communities to which we belong.

# Alphabetical List of Titles

# Acknowledgments

In writing *Lifelines,* I am clearly indebted to the long history of devotional literature and those who contributed to it. But I am also in debt to many contemporary conversationalists who had no intention of inspiring devotion and would be surprised to find their words, let alone their names, included in this series of meditations. Whether ancient or modern, I have found in both sources "something to grasp when there is danger of falling or being washed away." I am truly grateful.

I acknowledge especially the valuable role of editor Gwen played in the publication of this book. But that is the least of my debts to her. To quote Shakespeare I tally them in saying, without her,

I never writ, nor . . . ever lov'd.

## About the Author

For thirty years, Jake Kincaid was a parish minister. He lived and worked in North Carolina, Georgia, Virginia, and North Dakota. He holds a Bachelor of Science degree from Wake Forest University, a Master of Divinity degree from Duke University, where he concentrated his study in theology and psychology, and a Doctor of Philosophy degree in religious studies from Emory University. His primary interest has been in ethics, particularly in moral psychology. Jake and Gwen have been married for forty years. In retirement they live in Colorado.

38826702R00142

Made in the USA
Charleston, SC
17 February 2015